W. D

ANOTHER ARK TO BUILD

1800-WDF-1840 / 706-820-9755
www.WDFsermons.org

A Department of Wildwood Sanitarium, Inc.
www.WildwoodHealth.org

Published in the USA

March, 2016

ISBN: 978-1-944501-01-3

W. D. FRAZEE

ANOTHER ARK TO BUILD

WHO WAS W.D. FRAZEE?

It goes without saying that "a tall man casts a long shadow." And as the sun begins to set, the shadow grows even longer. W.D. Frazee (1906-1996) was educated in medical science at Loma Linda and in health evangelism by the legendary J.H.N. Tindall. In 1942, Elder Frazee and a faithful team of pioneers established Wildwood Sanitarium and Medical Missionary Institute where physicians, nurses, pastors, and laymen received practical training in medical evangelism.

From its humble beginnings, Wildwood has echoed the vision of the founders, nurtured in a prayerful study of the Scriptures and Spirit of Prophecy counsels. Today, it continues to educate medical missionary evangelistic workers from all over the world at its country outpost near Chattanooga, TN.

W. D. FRAZEE (1906-1996)

In 1985, during his retirement years, Elder Frazee established "Pioneers Memorial," which is now "W.D. Frazee Sermons". Thousands of audio files on various topics are distributed each year, and tens of thousands have gone around the world. We store, copy, and distribute the sermons of W.D. Frazee, E.A. Sutherland, Dr. Charles Thomas, and other pioneers of medical missionary work. Our goal is to remind this generation of the success and struggles of our self-supporting pioneers so that we may build on their experiences to finish the work in this generation.

You can view Elder Frazee's sermon titles available in audio and transcribed format on our website. We also have eBooks and many other special features on the site, including many free instant downloads. Visit us soon!

WDFsermons.org

CONTENTS

FOREWORD

Friday night vespers at Wildwood have always been the highlight of the week. As the sun is setting behind the mountains and the shadows lengthen in these green valleys, the sound of music and singing drifts heavenward from the little chapel. People come from many places to join in this worship service and to listen to the stirring vesper sermons given by Elder Frazee.

Seven of these have been printed and circulated as the *Sunset Series,* Numbers 1–7. Recently we felt the need of combining these and the little booklet *Overwhelming Surprise* into one book called *Another Ark to Build.* We pray that this volume may prove a blessing to all who read its pages.

Warren C. Wilson (1923-1989)
Executive Vice President
Wildwood Sanitarium Incorporated

PEACE AND SECURITY

T his is the first of a series of studies on the overwhelming surprise that is about to overtake the people of this world, what we can do about it, and how we can get ready for it. Our text is 1 Thessalonians 5:2-6, "For yourselves know perfectly that the day of the Lord so cometh as a thief in the night. For when they shall say, Peace and safety; then sudden destruction cometh upon them, as travail upon a woman with child; and they shall not escape. But ye, brethren, are not in darkness, that that day should overtake you as a thief. Ye are all the children of light, and the children of the day: we are not of the night, nor of darkness. Therefore let us not sleep, as do others; but let us watch and be sober."

Notice the words "sudden," "as a thief in the night." The day of the Lord is coming as a great surprise to the people of this world. Notice the comment on this in *Testimonies for the Church*, Vol. 8, page 37: "Soon an awful surprise is coming upon the inhabitants of the world," and again in *Testimonies*, Vol. 8, on page 28: "We who know the truth should be preparing for what is soon to break upon the world as *an overwhelming surprise.*"

Now, Paul says that the "brethren are not in darkness." God's children walk in the light, so that which surprises the world is not to be a surprise to us. We're to know what's coming and get ready for it; but unless we get ready for it, we will be taken in the snare. The reason for knowing what's ahead is so we can get ready.

There's a very interesting point in this scripture we've just read, as to the timing of the overwhelming surprise. "*When* they shall say, Peace and safety, *then* sudden destruction cometh upon them." Several of the modern translations put it, "Peace and security." In the public press these are the two great words, "Peace" and "Security." Phillips translates it, "You are well aware that the day of the Lord will come as unexpectedly as a burglary to a householder. When men are saying, 'Peace and security,' catastrophe will sweep down upon them." And the New English Bible:

"While they are talking of peace and security, all at once calamity is upon them." Isn't that what they're talking about right now, peace and security?

Let me call your attention to the two great world powers that are leading out and will continue to lead out in this talk of peace and security. One is the Pope of Rome and the other is the United States of America. When we turn to the book of Revelation, we find that the entire 13th chapter is devoted to presenting these two great powers. The first part deals with "the beast," and you and I know that leopard beast represents the papacy. In verse 3 we read of one of his heads being wounded to death, and the deadly wound being healed; and then what? "All the world wondered after the beast." Doubtless we all thought of that when the pope made that historic trip to the United Nations where he appeared as the ambassador of what? Peace. Peace—that's what the world is seeking.

The latter part of the 13th chapter of Revelation is devoted to the two-horned beast, and what does that represent? The United States of America. He is pictured in that chapter as joining hands with the papacy. And that is what is happening right before our eyes. But as the papacy—watch this point—as the papacy is taking the lead in the world quest for peace, the United States is, in a special sense, talking about that word "security." It's the great quest of this generation.

Notice how these two fit together and supplement each other. "Security." What are people thinking of? They're thinking about this present world. They're thinking about material possessions. They're thinking about how they are to be taken care of in sickness and old age. They're thinking about everything that will contribute to enjoying this present life. And we have now a program that's supposed to bring to the people of the United States "The Great Society" (another name for "Security"). But the United States is saying that this must be made available, not merely for this nation, but for all the peoples of the world. It's a great ambitious program.

The 13th chapter of Revelation shows the papacy and the United States of America joining hands in a great program that is to embrace the world: "All that dwell upon the earth shall worship him," that is, the papacy. And the two-horned beast is the inspiration to get all the world to do that. The 12th verse says he "causeth the earth and them that dwell therein to worship the first beast, whose deadly wound was healed." The reason that people are interested in these two great powers today is that they're hunting for peace and security. This is leading to combinations in every phase of life. Look at the Common Market in Europe. What's the basis of it? They want peace and security.

What is the reason for these labor unions, these trade associations? What's the basis of the ecumenical movement? Why are the churches trying to get together? Peace and security. And they will think that they have solved their problems by having these associations. With the papacy and the United States leading out, the whole world will think (for a very short time) that they either have this or almost have it.

Now, notice God's answer to all this in the 8th chapter of Isaiah. This is wonderful. The eye of the prophet, looking down the ages, saw our time. Isaiah 8:9, "Associate yourselves, O ye people, and ye shall be broken in pieces; and give ear, all ye of far countries [Here's the whole United Nations]: gird yourselves, and ye shall be broken in pieces; gird yourselves, and ye shall be broken in pieces. Take counsel together, and it shall come to not; speak the word, and it shall not stand: for God is with us." That is, with the remnant, those that keep the commandments of God and the faith of Jesus. Now notice, *they* are not to be in these combinations. That's the thing I want you to see. I read:

"For the Lord spake thus to me with a strong hand, and instructed me that I should not walk in the way of this people, saying, say ye not, A confederacy, to all them to whom this people shall say, A confederacy; neither fear ye their fear, nor be afraid." What's driving them? Fear! Fear of want, fear of war, fear of many things. So, with the Pope and the United States leading out, there must be combinations. The churches, the trade unions, the nations, the whole world must get together. But God's people are told in advance, "Say ye not, A confederacy." Don't fear their fear, don't get into that. "Sanctify the Lord of Hosts Himself; and let Him be your fear, and let Him be your dread. And He shall be for a sanctuary"—a place of security.

And so in the 16th and 17th verses He says, "Bind up the testimony, seal the law among My disciples." Here is the sealing message—the Sabbath put back in the law. "And I will wait upon the Lord, that hideth His face from the house of Jacob, and I will look for Him." While all the world is looking to confederacies, binding together in bundles in order to solve human problems and get peace and security, God says to His people, Don't get into that, look up. Look to the Lord. See how it is echoed in Isaiah 45:22: "Look unto Me, and be ye saved, all the ends of the earth; for I am God, and there is none else." Right here we have the answer to the problem. This is the faith that will save God's people and take us through the overwhelming surprise—*looking to God.* And it is the opposite course, looking to man, that makes it impossible for these world combinations to solve their problems. (The Great Society cannot solve the problems of man.) They are beyond human help. As the Spirit of Prophecy says, "They are struggling in vain to place business operations on a more secure basis." *Testimonies,* Vol. 9, p. 13. It is impossible for the governments of this world, following the plans they are using, to solve the material problems of men. It's even more impossible (if we may use such a term) for the papacy to solve the spiritual problems, because *the people are educated to look to man* instead of directly to Christ.

And so the message for today, as the Lord has given it to us in His Book, is "Behold your God." Notice how Jesus puts it in Luke 21. Pointing past the destruction of Jerusalem and the dark ages, He comes to the time of the end. In the 25th verse He says, "There shall be signs in the sun, and in the moon, and in the stars." Have we seen those? Yes. They are past. "And upon the earth distress of nations, with perplexity; the sea and the waves roaring; men's hearts failing them for fear, and for looking after those things which are coming on the earth." There's the fear again. That's what's driving them to these confederacies. There are thousands of people today who a few short years ago wouldn't have considered listening to the pope, that are ready to follow him now. Why? They are afraid of something that they think is far worse than the papacy.

Jesus says that men's hearts, in these last moments of time, will be "failing them for fear and for looking after those things which are coming on the earth." If we look where they look, we'll fear their fear, and we'll be drawn into these combinations. We will get into situations where we'll think that the only way out of trouble is to link up, one way or another, with some of these confederacies. And so what does Jesus say? "When these things begin to come to pass, *then look up*, and lift up your heads; for your redemption draweth nigh."

Soon, very soon, all the people in this world will be divided into just two camps—those who are looking to man, and those that are looking to God; those that are looking around them, and those that are looking up. Right there, the line is drawn. Now, the question is this: If God, who knows the future, sees that all this is coming, *what kind of training* will He be giving to His people? Will it not be a training to get them to look up, to look to God instead of to man? And how will He do this? Let us study this point.

If we get into difficulty and we find a certain way to solve the problem, and then that problem comes up again and we find the same way to solve our problem, do we not develop a habit as it goes on day after day? And would it not be difficult to change? Suppose I am thirsty. I think, 'Where will I get some water?' Somebody says, "There's a faucet in the kitchen. Just help yourself." Tomorrow I get thirsty again, and I think, 'Where will I get a drink? Oh, yes, I got a drink in the kitchen.' So I go again. And after I have done that a number of days, it's almost automatic, isn't it?

Now, if we get in the habit of having men solve our problems (whatever our problems are), what will be built into our characters? Dependence on whom? On man. And the devil has set every agency in operation to get us into that place, my dear friends. Whatever our problem is, whether it's a financial problem, a health problem, an emotional problem, a happiness problem, a religious problem—whatever it is—the billboards, the newspaper ads, the radio, and the TV are pouring ideas into the eyes and ears of the multitudes that there's some man or combination of men that can solve it all for us, especially if we will spend some money. That's the brainwashing that is going on. But God is conducting a different kind of school, and if we will listen, He will teach us something entirely different.

"Look unto Me and be ye saved, all the ends of the earth." And that's in the little things as well as in the big things.

Now, let me touch on a very practical point. This is in the book *Ministry of Healing*, page 486, "We are prone to look to our fellow men for sympathy and uplifting, instead of looking to Jesus." Yes, our natural tendency is to look to people. A little child does that and, of course, the little child should. Did you ever stub your toe and run, crying, "Mama, mama"? Is that all right for a little child to do? But how many "grown-up" people there are, my dear friends, that whatever trouble they get into, all they can think of is to run where? To some human being. And all of the "father confessors" are not in the Church of Rome. Ah, no. Nearly all the members of the human family, if they know anywhere to look for help, it is to some other human being. But if you and I are going to go through this overwhelming surprise and not be destroyed, *we will have to learn the lesson of looking to God instead of to men.*

And so, watch how God brings us to this lesson. "In his mercy and faithfulness, God often permits those in whom we place confidence to fail us, in order that we may learn the folly of trusting in man, and making flesh our arm." *Ministry of Healing*, p. 486. What is the only way that God can get us to learn that lesson? Ah, by allowing human beings to fail us. Did you ever get disappointed in some human being? What's the lesson of it all? "Cursed be the man that trusteth in man, and maketh flesh his arm. … Blessed is the man that trusteth in the Lord, and whose hope the Lord is." Jeremiah 17:5, 7.

Soon, as this overwhelming surprise breaks upon the world, as they see that they've been led to perdition by the dragon and the beast and the false prophet in the very act of talking of peace and security—oh, what a terrible awakening! And there will be a great terror that will spread from east to west, from pole to pole. The whole world will be in utter confusion. Earthquake, hailstones, terrible storms—all the elements of destruction will be turned loose. But hark! In the midst of all those warring elements, hear that song from the remnant: "God is our refuge and strength, a very present help in trouble. Therefore will not we fear, though the earth be removed." Psalm 46. Whatever happens, if men fail us, we're not building on them. If governments go down, our security is not in them. If the great religious leaders that have led the people to violate the law of God are overthrown and the whole world breaks up like the French revolution, our hope is in that Man in the sanctuary, Jesus Christ, who has said, "Look unto Me and be ye saved, all the ends of the earth."

Now, as I have said, He is training us for that very day. So today, if somebody disappoints us, let's remember what it's for. If it is a big disappointment, then we have a big lesson; if it's a little disappointment, we can have at least a little lesson. We are learning step by step not to build on man, but to build on Jesus Christ. And thus we are preparing to stand when great Babylon goes down like a great millstone cast into the depths of the sea. God's children will stand safe and secure because their anchor holds within the veil.

Dear Father, we thank Thee so much for the wonderful searchlight of prophecy illumining the road ahead. We choose to be those that are taught of God. While all the world is talking of peace and security, give us the true peace that comes in Thee and Thee alone. Give us the true security that is found in Thee and Thee alone. Thus may we be prepared for the disappointments of this world because we are anchored in heaven. For Jesus' sake. Amen.

PRICE OF PEACE

This morning we have our second lesson on the overwhelming surprise. We learned yesterday from 1 Thessalonians 5:2-6, "The day of the Lord so cometh as a thief in the night." Now, what will the people be saying when they are surprised? "Peace and safety," or, as we noted in other translations, "Peace and security." Does God intend that His people shall be engulfed in this great disaster? No! "Ye, brethren, are not in darkness, that that day should overtake you as a thief." We are to be saved from this overwhelming surprise.

In order to be saved, we must be prepared. We must understand what it is that's leading the world to these disasters, and we must be kept not merely from the end result, but from all the causes along the way. That is the purpose of these studies—to help us understand the basic causes that are leading the world to Armageddon.

We found yesterday in Isaiah 8 that, because of the fear of war and the fear of want, men are being led to extensive combinations. God plainly states that His people are not to enter into those confederacies. While the people of this world are talking confederacies, God's people will be looking where? Up to Him. That's the answer. "When we look to man, trouble grows. When we look to God, trouble goes." And we must learn that day by day in our own personal experience.

In the *Review and Herald* of November 4, 1965, there's a most interesting report of a statement made by a leading Roman Catholic Cardinal commenting on the pope's visit to the United Nations. He says, "It was a striking thing that no responsible voice has been raised in protest against the pope's visit. As recently as ten years ago, a papal visit to the United Nations would have been considered an onslaught and an invasion. But today, people are simply thrilled at the invitation of the pope to visit the UN and his willingness to do so. The reason for this is that people are so frightened of war that they are willing to try anything in desperation."

The cardinal spoke more truth than he realized. He put his finger right on the point. It's not some sincere turning toward God or toward religion that's leading the world to welcome the leadership of the papacy. What is it? Fear! We read in Isaiah 8, speaking to God's people, "Neither fear.ye their fear, nor be afraid." Are we afraid of war? No. Our Father is the king of this universe.

Notice the awful price that the people of this world are paying and will continue to pay, driven by their fear of war and fear of want. They are selling their souls for a mess of pottage, and they won't even get the mess of pottage. Esau got his lentils, but the people of this world are not even going to get that for which they sell their souls.

What are they selling to get peace? What are they going to lay down in order to accept the leadership of the pope of Rome? "All the world wondered after the beast." "All that dwell upon the earth shall worship him." Rev. 13:3, 8. Verse 12 shows that the United States is the one that leads out in causing all the world to accept this leadership of the papacy. What is the price of all this?

Proverbs 23:23 is right on the point. "Buy the truth, and sell it not." Can truth be bought and sold? Apparently. In Revelation 3:18, the True Witness says, "I counsel thee to buy of me gold tried in the fire … and white raiment … and eyesalve." The eyesalve is the discernment to know what's right and what's wrong. "Buy the truth." But once you've bought it, don't sell it! This is the terrible mistake the popular churches are making today. In reformation days, men like Luther, Zwingli, Calvin, Knox, and Wesley bought the truth, and it led them to separation from Rome. Today the Protestant churches are selling that glorious heritage. They are selling the truth which their fathers sacrificed everything to buy. That's the price they are paying to get back in favor with Rome in order that the pope may save them from a third world war.

Do you know that some of the creeds of Christendom are being revised in order to say this—watch this little change—no longer "the Bible *is* the Word of God," but the revised statement is, "The Bible *contains* the Word of God." Which do you believe? John 17:17 says, "Thy word is truth." The Bible *is* the Word of God. And there's an infinite difference between those two things, my friends. The inroads of modernism, of higher criticism, are weakening the faith of Protestants in the Scriptures. These have prepared the way to accept a human court of appeal, in the person of the papacy, to interpret what is truth.

The servant of the Lord tells us that the reason the book *Great Controversy* deals with the controversies of the past (the apostasy in the early ages, the rise of the papacy, the dark ages, and the reformation) is simply this: what has been, will be again. The last conflict into which we are even now entering is the climax of an age-long controversy. The issues are the same. The unseen forces are the same. And Rome that led the Christian world away from the Bible and set up the pope as the representative of Christ, Rome which in the dark ages slew the saints of God, is the same Rome under whose leadership all the world will be united to war against God's remnant.

On page 102 of *Great Controversy*, we are told about the experience of John Huss, who was burned at the stake because he became a reformer. He had been a papist, but as he studied the Bible, he came to a certain conclusion, and this is the thing I want you to notice. "God speaking in the Bible, and not the church speaking through the priesthood, is the one infallible guide." Here is the difference between Roman Catholicism on the one hand and true Protestantism on the other. And this is the truth which the Protestant world is selling that they may buy the favor of the papacy. And it is the fear of communism, the fear of atheism, the fear of war; yes, it is *fear* that is driving them to compromise.

Now notice the attitude of the true believers at the time the papacy was in process of formation. Here are the faithful few who would not go along with the Bishop of Rome and his hierarchy. "To secure peace and unity they were ready to make any concession consistent with fidelity to God; but they felt that even peace would be too dearly purchased at the sacrifice of principle. If unity could be secured only by the compromise of truth and righteousness, then let there be difference, and even war." *Great Controversy*, p. 45. This has been the position of Christ's followers in all ages—not to make trouble unnecessarily, not to push minor points of difference; but when it comes to a vital principle, no ecumenical idea justifies the selling of truth.

In the 17th chapter of John, we have the Saviour's earnest prayer for unity among His believers. But in that same prayer is this text we have already noticed, "Sanctify them through thy truth: thy word is truth." So the great question before Protestantism today is this, Which is more important, *truth* or *unity*? And there are thousands, yes millions, who are willing to sell the truth in order to secure unity. May I read this again: "To secure peace and unity they were ready to make any concession consistent with fidelity to God; but they felt that even peace would be too dearly purchased at the sacrifice of principle. If unity could be secured only by the compromise of truth and righteousness, then let there be difference, and even war."

Now, the next sentence is meaningful: "Well would it be for the church and the world if the principles that actuated those steadfast souls were revived in the hearts of God's professed people." The only thing, dear ones, which will keep us from being engulfed in this world movement for security and peace, the ecumenical movement, is a love for truth, so that we would rather have any war than give up truth. Our desire for peace must never degenerate into a willingness to compromise. And this must be manifest in the details of our personal lives. If we get in the habit of sacrificing principle so that we will be well thought of, *we are on the road to Rome.* No question about it. The remnant will be those who overcome by the blood of the Lamb, and by the word of their testimony; and who love not their lives unto the death. Revelation 12:11.

Speaking of this apostasy in the early ages, we read in *Great Controversy*, p. 49, "Almost imperceptibly the customs of heathenism found their way into the Christian church." How did this compromise come about? "Almost imperceptibly," that is, unnoticed like the twilight falls. Well, this was the twilight, and as the darkness settled upon the Christian world, it came "almost imperceptibly." That is the devil's game—to make the advances toward the world so small that the person who resists one of those advances is looked upon as silly, odd, unreasonable, stubborn.

And it isn't always in direct defiance to what God says that this compromise begins. "Rome began by enjoining what God had not forbidden, and she ended by forbidding what He had explicitly enjoined." *Great Con-*

troversy, p. 290. Rome began by telling people to do things that God had not plainly said they shouldn't do. Let me illustrate. Here is Christmas for the birth of Christ, Easter for the resurrection. Is there a verse in the Bible that says, don't celebrate the birthday of Christ, don't celebrate the day of His resurrection? No. So Rome began by introducing things that weren't expressly forbidden in the Bible. She ended by forbidding what He definitely told people to do, and the Sabbath is the great outstanding example. When men get in the habit of accepting as religious guides those who tell them to do *more* than the Bible says, they will inevitably end up following those guides to do what the Bible has forbidden. And this is the path that Protestantism, so-called, has been following for many years.

"As the Protestant churches have been seeking the favor of the world, false charity has blinded their eyes. They do not see but that it is right to believe good of all evil; and as the inevitable result, they will finally believe evil of all good." *Great Controversy*, p. 571. This is what is responsible for their current attitude toward the papacy. The popular thing in the Protestant churches today is to pat everybody on the back, and for the moment even Seventh-day Adventists are riding on the tide of popular favor—the ecumenical spirit. Many in the popular churches are ready to welcome Seventh-day Adventists as a part of the great Christian world. But the same spirit that leads them to welcome us is leading them to welcome Rome. We need to look very carefully at the hand that is stretched out to us, remembering that it is also offered to the Vatican. Let us not be flattered by the spirit of compromise. That hand which has been extended toward Rome will eventually be used, not to welcome us, but to smite us.

We need to look deep in our own hearts and see if there is anything in our souls that responds to this spirit of compromise. Are we weary of the war? Are we tired of the toil? Do we long for release from the conflict, and will we, in order to buy that release, sell the truth? That's the question. Will we give up conscientious convictions; will we soft-pedal the word of the Lord? God forbid!

Now, I mentioned that the world is not going to get the mess of pottage for which it sold out. Oh, my friends, this world that is selling the truth in order to buy peace from the pope of Rome, see what it's going to wake up and find! Revelation 19:19, "And I saw the beast, and the kings of the earth, and their armies, gathered together to make war..." This power that has supposedly led the world to peace is going to lead it instead to war! This is the war against God. "I saw the beast, and the kings of the earth, and their armies, gathered together to make war against Him that sat on the horse, and against His army." And so, while the nations of this world are following after the phantom of peace, they are led to the greatest war of the ages.

Revelation 16:13, 14: "I saw three unclean spirits like frogs come out of the mouth of the dragon, and out of the mouth of the beast, and out of the mouth of the false prophet. For they are the spirits of devils, working miracles, which go forth unto the kings of the earth and of the whole world, to gather them to the battle of that great day of God Almighty." Notice this in *Testimonies*, Vol. 7, p. 182, "The world is filled with storm and war and variance. Yet under one head—the papal power—the people will unite to oppose God in the person of His witnesses."

For a short time, this world is going to be united. The next sentence says, "This union is cemented by the great apostate." Under one head—the papal power—all the nations will unite to oppose God in the person of His witnesses. Where will you and I be? On one side or the other. We'll either be with Jesus and his remnant church, conscientiously standing for what the Word of God says—all 10 of His Commandments—or else we'll be with the great popular movement which has sold the truth in order to buy peace. Remember, they are going to sell the truth, but they are not going to get peace. "*When they shall say, Peace and safety; then sudden destruction cometh upon them ... and they shall not escape.*" 1 Thessalonians 5:3.

Oh, friends, when the voice of God ends the captivity of His people, when His law is seen in the sky, there will be a terrible awakening among all these churches that have combined together in compromise to buy peace. The union which the great apostate has cemented will fall to pieces. The great city will be divided into three parts and every man's hand will rise up against the hand of his brother. Read the awful picture in Revelation 16, and Jeremiah 25, and in *Great Controversy* in the chapter titled

"The Desolation of the Earth." See the breakdown of civilization. See the churches in chaos and the members tearing the ministers and the priests limb from limb. The whole world is going to be plunged into the scenes of the French Revolution. Peace? Oh, no. Not peace. Sacrifice of the truth can never lead to peace.

And so it means much to you and to me to answer the question, Do we love the truth enough to die for it, enough to live for it? Or are we willing to compromise?

Dear Lord, write upon our hearts Thy truth. Deep in our souls, put a love for it so that we would rather die than sacrifice one principle. For Jesus' sake. Amen.

The Trap

"The day of the Lord so cometh as a thief in the night"—suddenly, unexpectedly. And what will "they" be talking about? "Peace and safety." "Then sudden destruction cometh upon them. ... They shall not escape." 1 Thessalonians 5:2, 3. But all this is told us so that *we* can escape.

I would like to stress this important fact: the light that we have is not light concerning future dates. Christ says, "The Son of man cometh at an hour when ye think not." Luke 12:40. So the light that God has given us is not to enable us to look ahead and say that on a certain date Christ will come, or probation will close, or great Babylon will go down. We have the knowledge that we are in the time of the end, but we have been there for many years. We have some knowledge of the sequence of coming events.

But the great light that God has given you and me is the light on how to avoid the experience, the state of mind, which gets Babylon into this awful crisis. They say "peace and safety, peace and security," and, as we studied in our last lesson, they are willing to sell the truth in order to try to buy peace. This explains the great interest in the pope's coming over to the United Nations. That's why all the world wonders after the beast. They think that he's going to keep them from this terrible atomic war. So they are willing to give up their doctrinal differences. They are willing to sacrifice truth in an endeavor to get the peace that unity is supposed to bring. But, as we have found, they will have a terrible disappointment.

They are not only saying "peace" but "security." Those are the two great words on the lips of people today, "peace and security." And, as the pope is supposed to work out the peace, so the United States is being looked to as the great world leader to work out this problem of security.

In Luke 21 are the words of Jesus on the Mount of Olives to His disciples. He's warning them, just as Paul warns in Thessalonians, of the approaching crisis. After speaking (beginning in verse 25) of the signs in the sun, moon, and stars, "and upon the earth distress of nations, with perplexity … men's hearts failing them for fear, and for looking after those things which are coming on the earth," and picturing the coming of Jesus, He gives the warning (in verse 34 and onward), "Take heed to yourselves." He's talking to His disciples, but also to you and me. "Take heed to yourselves, lest at any time your hearts be overcharged" (overloaded, overburdened) "with surfeiting, and drunkenness, and cares of this life, and so that day come upon you unawares." (That's the theme—this sudden, unexpected calamity, this overwhelming surprise!) But what is it that leads the people of the world into that very condition? It is the way they eat, the way they drink, the way they work, the way they play, the way they live. It isn't that they don't have a calendar or a schedule. Their whole way of life leads to that terrible disappointment at Armageddon; that awful disillusionment, as all that they have worked for crumbles to ruin before their eyes. "The cities of the nations fell," John says. Everything is going to be in ruins. So Jesus says, "Take heed to yourselves," lest you get caught in this trap; not merely (and I keep emphasizing this) the fact that it will come on a day when you might not expect it. No! The trap is earlier than Armageddon.

"For as a snare"—that word means "trap." "For as a trap shall it come on all them that dwell on the face of the whole earth." All who make this world their home are going to be caught in the trap, and they're getting caught now. That's what we need to see.

So, Jesus warns in the 36th verse, "Watch." Not watch the calendar to find out which day Jesus is going to come, and then run! "Watch ye therefore, and pray always, that ye may be accounted worthy to escape all these things that shall come to pass, and to stand before the Son of man." Thank God, dear friends, we can live in this world without being contaminated by it. We can walk in and out and around all these traps and not get caught. Isn't that wonderful? That's what God wants. That's His plan, and if we'll listen to Him, He will keep us.

To many people of this world, security means money and the things that money can buy. People want money because it gives them "status." They want to "be somebody." They desire an expensive automobile so that, as they ride down the street, their neighbors view them enviously. But the trap is not the car, the expensive house, or the extravagant furniture. Oh, no! It is the state of mind that wants these things and tries to get them. And for one that succeeds, there are a hundred others caught in the same trap that never get the bait. But hook and bait together, or hook without the bait, they're all hooked.

Notice how good God is to warn us about these traps: "But godliness with contentment is great gain. For we brought nothing into this world, and it is certain we can carry nothing out." 1 Timothy 6:6, 7. Whether we go by grave or translation route, we are not going to carry any of the gold of this world, any of the fine cars or expensive furniture. "And having food and raiment let us be therewith content." 1 Timothy 6:8. Most people are not content, and it doesn't make any difference whether they're poor or whether they are millionaires, they are not content. They're in the trap of discontent, restlessness, selfishness, envy, covetousness. Are *we* content? Well, if we are in the light, we are, friends. We all have food, and clothes, and a place to live. And we are to "be therewith content." Praise God!

Now, to the point: "But they that will be rich" (that is, those that are striving to be rich—not merely the ones that succeed, mind you, but those that want to be rich), "fall into temptation and a snare." This is the same word we read in Luke 21 meaning "trap." As a "trap," it is coming. And those that will be rich, those that are determined to be rich, fall right into the trap. "But they that will be rich fall into temptation and a snare, and into many foolish and hurtful lusts, which drown men in destruction and perdition." 1 Timothy 6:9. They get drowned.

You know, a man could drown in honey as well as in the ocean. It would be a sweet death, but he would be just as dead, wouldn't he? And some people are drowning in the foolish and hurtful lusts of this world. Shall we envy them? Oh, no! Rather pity them, pray for them.

"For the love of money is the root of all evil: which while some coveted after, they have erred from the faith, and pierced themselves through with many sorrows. But thou, O man of God, flee these things; and follow after righteousness, godliness, faith, love, patience, meekness." 1 Timothy 6:10, 11. You see, all the way through these verses, Jesus is pointing out the trap so that we may avoid it. He is pointing out the way of light that we may walk in it. Let's do it, what do you say?

Something is happening in this world to really get people in the trap. Never in all the history of the ages have so many people been in debt. Look at these cars going up and down the highway. How many are paid for? Very few. And by the time they get paid for, they must be traded in and the cycle repeated. But that's only the beginning. It isn't just automobiles, but refrigerators, radios, TV's, Hi-fi's, furniture, taking trips, anything. Borrow money, start paying it off; borrow money, keep paying it off.

God has some advice for us in Romans 13:8. "Owe no man any thing." Oh, surely not! Well, there is an exception. "Owe no man any thing, but to love one another." Yes, we owe love to everybody, and we are to keep paying on that all the time. God doesn't want His children to be in debt. Why not? He wants them to be happy. Debts don't make people happy. Many a soul commits suicide because suddenly a mountain of debt has fallen like an avalanche upon him. Oh, how it gnaws at the vitals. Somebody says, "Well, it doesn't seem to bother some people." More is the pity, friends. In their case, debt has worked like an anesthetic, like one of these tranquilizers. But all that drug action is artificial and injurious.

We have had some counsel on this point. "Let all now seek most earnestly to avoid the mistakes of the past. Let them guard themselves as with a fence of barbed wire against the inclination to go into debt." *Testimonies*, Vol. 7, p. 236. Put up a barbed wire fence! Now, lest some should misunderstand, there are cases where the Lord has plainly indicated that it is right to go into debt to get a facility for His work started. Sister White, at times, borrowed money and even paid interest in order to build a meeting house or to get a sanitarium established. In those cases, she had security to give to make sure that the debt would be paid. But those exceptions do not abolish the rule. The rule is, "Owe no man any thing." If you are in debt, get out. Then keep out. *And that is one way to avoid the trap.*

Let me illustrate. Here is a man who hears God's message of truth. He wants to keep the Sabbath, but if he does, he's going to lose his job. Now, that was hard enough 50 years ago, but there's something about the situation today that makes it much harder. There was a time that a man could step out to keep the Sabbath, and if he lost his job, at least whatever he had was his own. That time is largely gone. Today, the man that steps out to keep the Sabbath and loses his job runs the risk of losing everything that he has invested in property, in furniture, in automobile. He's under that shadow of debt. Do you see how the devil has engineered things to make it difficult for people to make a move of faith? He's stacked up the odds against them.

It is the same thing in doing a work for God. Here comes the call to somebody to work for Jesus, perhaps to go into the colporteur work, perhaps to go into some other phase of self-supporting labor for the Lord. But, he's in debt. Dear friends, if we knew how many people this morning are working to get out of debt so they can go into the Lord's work, the figure would astonish us. But the devil is a great trapper and once he has them in that trap, he doesn't like to let them go.

I've heard more than one young man say, "As soon as I can get a car," or "As soon as I can do this or that, then I'm going to give my full time to the work." So they go into debt, and oh, how they are held, sometimes forever. Sometimes they finally get loose, seldom as soon as they think they will. There's something about it that's a trap.

Another reason people want money is for indulgence. A man thinks if he has money he can buy anything he wants to eat, he can buy anything he wants to drink. He can take it easy; or if he's interested in lust, he thinks he can indulge himself in that. Whatever his particular appetite or passion, money is the means to satisfy it. But Jesus says they *drown themselves* in those foolish and hurtful lusts. Why friends, instead of money being sought after because it is the key to self-indulgence, that's one of the great reasons to give it a second look.

The reason some people are going to be in heaven is that God, in mercy, let them be poor so they wouldn't have the money to indulge themselves so much. If God has given us a measure of poverty, it may be it will keep our brains clear so we can think and avoid the traps of the devil.

In our first study, we noted that this passion for peace and security is leading men into confederacies and associations. Isaiah 8 says to the nations and the people of this world that if they indulge in that solution of their problem, they will find only disappointment. God says to His children, Don't walk in that road.

"The world is a theater; the actors, its inhabitants, are preparing to act their part in the last great drama. With the great masses of mankind, there is *no unity, except as men confederate to accomplish their selfish purposes.* God is looking on." *Testimonies*, Vol. 8, p. 27. You notice that the only unity they have is union to get their own way. Each man that enters into a confederacy thinks, This is the way to advantage myself. "The world has not been given into the hands of men, though God is permitting the elements of confusion and disorder to bear sway for a season. A power from beneath is working to bring about the last great scenes in the drama—Satan coming as Christ, and working with all deceivableness of unrighteousness in those who are binding themselves together in secret societies. Those who are yielding to the passion for confederation are working out the plans of the enemy. The cause will be followed by the effect.

"Transgression has almost reached its limit. Confusion fills the world and a great terror is soon to come upon human beings. The end is very near. We who know the truth should be preparing for what is soon to break upon the world as an *overwhelming surprise.*" *Testimonies*, Vol. 8, pp. 27, 28.

How can we prepare? By avoiding the trap: the trap of confederacies with the world, the trap of this ecumenical idea, the trap of debt, the trap of wanting to be rich, the trap of these labor unions, the trap of living for selfish ease, selfish pleasure, selfish indulgence. Avoid all that. Jesus says, Watch and pray, and don't let your heart get overcharged with eating and drinking and the cares of this world. It's coming as a snare. "But you, brethren, are not in darkness that that day should overtake you as a thief." You're not to get caught in that trap. You're walking in the light: the light of love, the light of unselfish ministry, the light of dedication to the unfinished task, the light of looking to Jesus instead of men. Oh friends, haven't we a wonderful Saviour and a wonderful program, a wonderful way of life! Let us thank God every day for it and make Him happy by letting Him know that we appreciate it.

Dear Father, seal to our hearts the lesson of the morning. Help us never to envy the rich and those who are trying to be rich. Help us not to get caught in these confederacies that men are forming in the endeavor to get their own way. Keep us, Lord, from being deceived by that man on the Tiber, and keep us from being deceived by the dreams of wealth and security that are lulling this poor nation to sleep, on the brink of doom. Help us to share with others the light of Thy love. For Jesus' sake. Amen.

PREPARATION

This morning, as we study about the overwhelming surprise, let us notice the issue that prophecy puts the searchlight on: "And he causeth all, both small and great, rich and poor, free and bond, to receive a mark in their right hand, or in their foreheads: and that no man might buy or sell, save he that had the mark, or the name of the beast, or the number of his name." Rev. 13:16, 17. Here is a clear prediction that a mark is the mark of apostasy, the false rest day, the change of the Sabbath from Saturday, the seventh day, to Sunday, the first day. That will be the issue.

"The Sabbath will be the great test of loyalty; for it is the point of truth especially controverted … While one class, by accepting the sign of submission to earthly powers, receive the mark of the beast, the other, choosing the token of allegiance to divine authority, receive the seal of God." *Great Controversy*, p. 605. Everyone will receive the seal or the mark. While the day in each case is the sign, the sign represents an experience, an experience of total allegiance to God on the one hand, or total submission to man on the other. And the way to prepare for this overwhelming surprise is to get in the habit of looking heavenward to Jesus rather than depending on men.

Now, notice what's going to happen to the people that depend on men. "That no man might buy or sell, save he that had the mark." Those who are depending on men will be forced, literally forced, into submission. This is a very interesting text because it's quite in harmony with the spirit of the present generation. Today, in the United States, it would be unpopular to advocate a death decree against people who keep Saturday. At the moment, the atmosphere is one of the ecumenical spirit, of pulling together for peace. But on the other hand, economic sanctions as they are called, are looked upon as proper coercive weapons. The United Nations has been called upon at various times to enforce sanctions. People are prepared for the idea that if there are those who will not cooperate, perhaps the best way to deal with them is just to cut off their bread and butter.

You can see that if we, God's children, are to be prepared, there are two things that we need to get settled. One is that we are willing for God to provide for us in as meager or generous a way as He sees best, and the other is that we will do our best to work with Him to provide in preparation for that day.

"The Protestant world have set up an idol Sabbath in the place where God's Sabbath should be, and they are treading in the footsteps of the papacy. For this reason I see the necessity of the people of God moving out of the cities into retired country places, where they may cultivate the land and raise their own produce." *Selected Messages*, Vol. 2, p. 359. Now, that's just as plain as language could be. Over this issue of the Sabbath-Sunday question comes the last great crisis, and *for this reason*, the Lord's messenger says, "I see the necessity of the people of God moving out of the cities into retired country places, where they may cultivate the land and raise their own produce. Thus they may bring their children up with simple, healthful habits. I see the necessity of making haste to get all things ready for the crisis." *Ibid.* Written in 1897, this is one of the early calls to get our people out of the cities into retired country places.

Remember, the keynote of this series of lessons is that God's people, children of light, are not going to be overtaken by the overwhelming surprise. We are to be preparing for it. Noah did that before the flood. The people back there were just as much surprised as though there had been no warning. They ate and drank and married and gave in marriage until the day that Noah entered into the ark. They "knew not until the flood came, and took them all away; so shall also the coming of the Son of man be." Matt. 24:39. The world is going to be just as surprised today as though they had never been warned; and yet God in His love is warning them, and will continue to warn them, until every soul gets the warning, just as in Noah's day. The people who heed the warning, God's remnant people, along with keeping the Sabbath, will break loose from the confederacies. They will break loose from the situations that would make it impossible for them to obey God's law, and they will establish themselves out in the county in "retired places" where they can "raise their own produce," and where they can "bring their children up with simple, healthful habits." Here are the two great reasons for getting out in the country. One is the pressure over the Sunday law; the other is that we may have the spiritual help of contact with nature and being away from the crime and vice of the cities. Thank the Lord He has warned us.

"We are not to locate ourselves where we will be forced into close relations with those who do not honor God.... A crisis is soon to come in regard to the observance of Sunday.... We are to place ourselves where we can carry out the Sabbath commandment in its fullness and we are to be careful not to place ourselves where it will be hard for ourselves and our children to keep the Sabbath.... There are troublous times before us." *Selected Messages*, Vol. 2, p. 359. You see how the warning is given in various words again and again.

One of the agencies that will have a part in bringing about this boycott over the Sunday law is the labor unions. In recent years we have seen the churches, both Catholic and Protestant, linking up with the labor unions in the drive for Sunday laws. Notice this statement, "The trades unions will be one of the agencies that will bring upon this earth a time of trouble such as has not been since the world began." *Selected Messages*, Vol. 2, p. 142.

Now, that fits right into the prophecy in Revelation 13. It is an economic pressure. Later, of course, there will be a death decree fulfilling the 15th verse. But, at first, the world will think that Seventh-day Adventists can be brought to their knees in submission by simply refusing to let them buy and sell. So, we have much to learn along that line. One thing, as we have already read here, is to disassociate ourselves from the associations of this world. There is warning after warning on this. "The work of the people of God is to prepare for the events of the future, which will soon come upon them with blinding force." Ibid. There's the overwhelming surprise, you see. "In the world gigantic monopolies will be formed. Men will bind themselves together in unions that will wrap them in the folds of the enemy. A few men will combine to grasp all the means to be obtained in certain lines of business. Trades unions will be formed, and those who refuse to join these unions will be marked men.... The trades unions and confederacies of the world are a snare. Keep out of them, and away from them, brethren. Have nothing to do with them." *Selected Messages*, Vol. 2, p. 142. And notice, looking into the future, on page 144, "Those who claim to be the children of God are in no case to bind up with the labor unions that are formed or that shall be formed. This the Lord forbids. Cannot those who study the prophecies see and understand what is before us?"

See how the different parts of the world's program all fit together, and the different parts of God's program all fit together? If you were the devil and you were trying to get people into these confederacies, where would you have them live? In the cities. But if you had Heaven's point of view and you were trying to keep people away from these confederacies, where would you have them live? Out in the country. It is just that simple.

"There followed another angel, saying, Babylon is fallen, is fallen, that great city, because she made all nations drink of the wine of the wrath of her fornication." Rev. 14:8. "He cried mightily with a strong voice, saying, Babylon the great is fallen.... And I heard another voice from heaven, saying, Come out of her, my people." Rev. 18:2-4. I want to ask you something. Where does the person have to be that says, "Come out?" He has to be out. If we are partakers of the spirit of this world, if we are in the unions and combinations of this world, how can we give the message, "Come out?" And if our hearts, like Lot's poor wife, are in Sodom, how can we urge anybody to leave it?

It's true we must visit the cities to give them that message, but it will be to say, "Come home with me." That's what Enoch did, didn't he? Oh friends, let us get that spirit to say, "Come out."

But we will never be able to give that message as we should unless we have a true understanding of the values of country living and a real appreciation of the blessings of country life. Lot didn't have that. How many converts did he get as he preached there? Not one! He wasn't enthusiastic about leaving Sodom. He went down there in the first place because of the pressure from his family. He "pitched his tent toward Sodom." Gen. 13:12. He probably had no intention of moving in, but it seemed more convenient as time went on. He would have greater advantages commercially and socially; and it worked out that way. He was an honored man in

Sodom. I suspect he thought it was a fine thing to have that influence that he could use for God; but did it accomplish anything as far as the people of Sodom were concerned? Not a thing, friends. Why? Because he had the city mind. He didn't have the country mind.

How different was Abraham's contact with Sodom. Recorded in Genesis 14 is the wonderful experience when he saved the lives of the people and the king of Sodom. He was respected and honored as he lived out in the country under the oaks at Mamre, away from all that sin and vice for which Sodom had even then become proverbial. Oh friends, do you see how vital it is that we cherish the privileges, the royal privileges, of living in the country, rather than thinking it is a sacrifice?

When Lot was called out of Sodom, the angels of God had to pull him out—literally. Then the Lord said, "Lot, see that mountain.? Flee! Escape for thy life!" "Oh, no!" he says, "I can't go up there. Some evil would overtake me." He had become so used to city streets and city conveniences, he was afraid of country life. So he picked out a little city and he said, "Couldn't you let me go there? Won't you spare that one?" And the merciful Lord said, "Alright." You see what I mean, friends. He didn't understand. He didn't appreciate the goodness of God in making it possible for him to live in the country. He went to Zoar, but soon left it to live in a cave. Zoar was destroyed as Sodom had been. And there is recorded the awful story of the immoral conduct of his daughters. They had learned it down there in the city, just as young people are learning it in the cities of today. What a terrible record; but it's written there for us, because Jesus says, "As it was in the days of Lot…thus shall it be in the day when the Son of man is revealed." Luke 17:28, 30.

And that's the great problem today, friends. People are so wedded to these advantages—social, political, commercial, educational, and all the rest—that it's hard to get them to break loose. But I want to read you something: "*But ere long there will be such strife and confusion in the cities that those who wish to leave them will not be able.* We must be preparing for these issues. This is the light that is given me." *Selected Messages*, Vol. 2, p. 142. Again and again in these references we catch that repeated refrain, "we must be preparing."

One of the greatest things that we need to do to resist these pressures is to get our minds in shape so that we think as God thinks instead of the way the world thinks. Jesus came down here and took our poverty that we might share Heaven's riches, and those who get the spirit of this message will be willing to be poor in order that they may save themselves and their children, rather than be rich in this world for a few days.

"Who will be warned? We say again, 'Out of the cities.' *Do not consider it a great deprivation*, that you must go into the hills and mountains, but seek for that retirement where you can be alone with God, to learn His will and way.... I urge our people to make it their lifework to seek for spirituality. Christ is at the door. This is why I say to our people, 'Do not consider it a privation when you are called to leave the cities and move out into the country places.'" *Selected Messages*, Vol. 2, pp. 355, 356.

If we consider it a privation to live in the country, we won't stay there long. Sooner or later, we'll be back in the city. We will pay our dollar down and so much a month for who knows how long in order to get this and that and the other thing. We'll have to get in the harness. We'll have to be driven by the lash. We'll have to be chained like the galley slave and work our lives away so that our children can have all these so-called marvelous advantages and conveniences that modern city life offers. But all the while, out in the country with God are rich treasures in contact with nature: the glow of sunrise, unobscured by the city's smog, the glories of the flowers, the trees, the lake, the mountains, the fellowship of working with God instead of just working with machines! Shall we count our blessings? Shall we rejoice in the privileges of royalty? And meanwhile, not as hermits, but as Enochs, as evangelists, let's reach out and say to the weary multitudes, to all who will listen, "Come out."

Dear Lord, put in our hearts such a view of what's ahead as shall stir us to do our best to gather in Thy remnant in this last hour. For Jesus' sake. Amen.

THE SIGN

In the September 1965 issue of *The U.S. Catholic Magazine*, there appeared an article entitled, "Why the Seventh-day Adventists are Succeeding." This is an interesting day, when the Roman Catholic Church is taking cognizance of this little denomination. Written in the ecumenical spirit, it raises the question, "What can we learn from our separated brethren? What can we learn from our Adventist friends?" It praises the Seventh-day Adventist Church for its zeal, for its church school system, for its health reform message and the results as revealed in our comparative freedom from lung cancer and some other diseases.

The author says: "Unlike most Christian denominations, the Seventh-day Adventist Church has barely been touched by the current ecumenical movement." I trust that will continue to be so. Continuing in the article:

"Roman Catholicism fares rather poorly in Adventist preaching and literature. Some Adventist authors carry on an old-fashioned vendetta against the Church of Rome, whose popes were responsible for changing the observance of the Sabbath from Saturday to Sunday and hereby heading Christendom down the road to apostasy." Obviously, that's simply this author reflecting what he feels is the Adventist view. He doesn't think that the change of the Sabbath from Saturday to Sunday headed Christendom down the road to apostasy, but he's representing the Adventist position.

Now listen carefully as I read: "Most Protestants as well as Catholics reject the Adventist interpretation of the Sabbath commandment as demanding the observance of Saturday. Nevertheless we might profit from an examination of how the Adventists try to keep their Sabbath holy. For the devout Adventist the Sabbath begins at sundown Friday as it does for the orthodox Jews. Meals are prepared on Friday so that food preparation need not take up the wife's time on the Sabbath. Saturday morning is spent in church and Sabbath School. The rest of the day is devoted to Bible reading and study, simple family recreation such as nature walks, prayer, and discussing Bible topics with friends. The radio and the TV are silent until the end of the Sabbath at sundown on Saturday."

Isn't that a beautiful picture of Seventh-day Adventists observing the Lord's holy day? God help us to live it out every Sabbath.

Now, I go back to the article: "Could we contrast this observance of the Sabbath with that which characterizes the conduct of millions of Christians? In too many homes Sunday may be a day free from regular employment but it is really just another day of the week. If we take a stroll through many neighborhoods we will see Christians painting their homes, washing the car, hanging storm windows or screens, carrying on various do-it-yourself projects. We know that shopping centers and stores could not make a profit on Sunday if millions of Christians did not choose that day of the week to buy furniture, automobiles, appliances, groceries, and clothing. We profess to be shocked that the Soviets deliberately erased the religious significance of Sunday in order to undermine the role of religion in the lives of the Russian people. Have we not done much the same thing in the United States and often in defiance of the laws designed to preserve the values of a day of rest? Our Adventist friends remind us that the Sabbath was not given only to a band of desert peoples centuries ago but to each generation of men. God asks that all men set apart one day out of seven to His service as well as to the recreation of the human body and spirit. The author of man's nature knew that such a day was essential to mans' spiritual, emotional, and physical well-being. We not only disobey His commandment but we flirt with personal disaster when we ignore the significance of the Sabbath. As Catholics we have often aimed at a minimal observance of the Lord's day; we attend Mass and avoid servile work, broadly defined. Perhaps the Adventists can remind us that the creative and holy observance of the day demands more than this bare minimum."

Very interesting, isn't it? Then the author speaks of our extensive welfare program not limited merely to Adventists. He mentions our Dorcas and welfare societies and the fact that Adventists don't believe in killing, that they are non-combatants. Then he says, "We can see that the decision to become an Adventist would not be made lightly. The convert would be expected to tithe his income, attend Sabbath services every week, abstain from all unnecessary work on the Sabbath, forego liquor and tobacco, educate his children in parochial schools, avoid dancing, card-playing, and movies, give up cosmetics and jewelry, sever any connection with a secret society. Yet the Adventists seem to be purposeful, contented people who derive a deep satisfaction from their religion."

Isn't that wonderful? I hope that those responsible for taking members into the church will note that this is the standard that our Catholic friends think converts are accepting in coming into the Seventh-day Adventist Church. There are details here that sometimes need emphasis.

Now, back to the article. After telling about the history of our movement, how it arose back in the 1844 days with William Miller, how they were disappointed and then decided they wouldn't set any more dates but look for the imminent return of Christ—"To this basic doctrine of Adventism the tiny New England congregation added the belief that Christians should observe the Old Testament Sabbath rather than Sunday which had been designated by an early pope. The role of the pope in changing the observance has given the movement an anti-Catholic orientation. Many Adventists seem to consider the pope to be the Anti-Christ."

Notice how, from the beginning to the end, the Sabbath stands out as the great landmark of this movement. In all this, I seem to hear the echo of *The Great Controversy*, page 605, "The Sabbath will be the great test of loyalty; for it is the point of truth especially controverted.... While one class, by accepting the sign of submission to earthly powers, receive the mark of the beast, the other, choosing the token of allegiance to divine authority, receive the seal of God." There we have it.

Notice what the *Convert's Catechism of Catholic Doctrine*, page 50, says on this matter: "Which is the Sabbath day? Saturday is the Sabbath day. Why do we observe Sunday instead of Saturday? We observe Sunday instead of Saturday because the Catholic Church transferred the solemnity from Saturday to Sunday." Very clear and right to the point.

Cardinal Gibbons, in his well-known book, *The Faith of our Fathers*, page 111: "But you may read the Bible from Genesis to Revelation and you will not find a single line authorizing the sanctification of Sunday. The Scriptures enforce the religious observance of Saturday, a day which we never sanctify."

You see, this Sabbath question is more than the matter of a day. It is the question of whether the church speaking through the pope, or Christ speaking through the Bible, is the real authority.

Notice this book put out by the Paulist Press in New York City, *The Question Box*, page 179: "What Bible authority is there for changing the Sabbath from the seventh to the first day of the week? Who gave the pope the authority to change a command of God?" That's the question. Now, here's their answer: "If the Bible is the only guide for the Christian, then the Seventh-day Adventist is right in observing the Saturday with the Jew. But Catholics learn what to believe and do from the divine infallible authority established by Jesus Christ, the Catholic Church." And on this issue comes the last great battle. I repeat: It is more than a day. It's a philosophy of life. Are we looking to men or to Christ? Are we looking to human ordinances, or to the eternal unchangeable law of God?

"And after these things I saw four angels standing on the four corners of the earth, holding the four winds of the earth, that the wind should not blow on the earth, nor on the sea, nor on any tree." Rev. 7:1. What are those winds? Strife, war, confusion, persecution—all the elements of destruction. What are the angels doing? Holding them. But, in the vision they seem about ready to relax their hold and let the winds blow. But John sees another angel "ascending from the east, having the seal of the living God: and he cried with a loud voice to the four angels, to whom it was given to hurt the earth and the sea, saying, Hurt not the earth, neither the sea, nor the trees, till we have sealed the servants of our God in their foreheads." Rev. 7:2, 3.

Here is the sealing of the remnant just before the last great crisis. As we have already studied, that awful storm of destruction is going to come over this world suddenly, unexpectedly. In Revelation 7 we see what's holding back that awful overwhelming surprise. The angels of God are holding it back until the servants of God are sealed in their foreheads. You and I know what that seal is. What is it? The Sabbath. "I gave them my sabbaths, to be a sign between me and them, that they might know that

I am the Lord that sanctify them." "Hallow my sabbaths; and they shall be a sign between me and you, that ye may know that I am the Lord your God." Ezekiel 20:12, 20. So the Sabbath is the central feature in God's holy law which is to be imprinted so deeply into the minds and hearts of the remnant that nothing can shake them.

"Just as soon as the people of God are sealed in their foreheads—it is not any seal or mark that can be seen, but a settling into the truth both intellectually and spiritually, so they cannot be moved—just as soon as God's people are sealed and prepared for the shaking, it will come. Indeed, it has begun already; the judgments of God are now upon the land, to give us warning, that we may know what is coming." E. G. White, *S.D.A. Bible Commentary*, Vol. 6, p. 1161.

The judgments of God with the resulting shaking have begun, and yet the great fulfillment is future. These winds are blowing a bit as the angels loosen their hold, but the blowing of the winds with no restraint— the great time of trouble, the universal persecution, the worldwide strife— these are yet future. And these winds are held in check until what? *Until you and I get settled in the truth.*

Somebody says, "Well, I'm settled." Are you? How much can you stand? Can you stand up in an 80-mile-an-hour wind? What about a hurricane, 120 miles an hour, 150 miles? Ah, my dear friends, the winds are going to blow, and it's going to mean something to the universe of God to look down upon this little planet and watch the 144,000 stand when the howling hurricane is turned loose against the people of God. "The dragon was wroth with the woman, and went to make war with the remnant of her seed, which keep the commandments of God, and have the testimony of Jesus Christ." Rev. 12:17.

Now is the time to prepare for what is soon to come upon the world as an overwhelming surprise. It is very clear that the central feature of this preparation is to get the Sabbath sealed in our foreheads so deeply that nothing can efface it. We see it is recognized by the Catholics as the great separating point between their movement and ours. God recognizes it, makes it a subject of prophecy—the seal in the seventh chapter of Revelation going into the minds of the remnant; the mark of the beast in the 13th chapter being enforced by the economic and other pressures upon all the rest of the world. And in that issue, all the world will be divided into two great classes. Most will take the mark of the beast because they have been preparing for it. They have the habit of accepting the rule of man instead of the rule of God. They have the habit of accepting "peace and security" instead of truth and liberty. But God's people have learned to love His law, and the Saviour who is the Author of the law; and as a result they come to the place where the truth, the Sabbath, is so identified with them and they with it, that it is impossible to separate them. The only way to get rid of those strange ideas would be to kill them! And this is what the world is eventually going to attempt.

In Isaiah 58, I want you to see what it is that's going to enable us to have that kind of settling into the truth. This great medical missionary chapter is also the great chapter of Sabbath reform. The remnant are pictured as raising up the foundations of many generations. They are restorers, reformers. In the 13th verse the promise to them is, "If thou turn away thy foot from the Sabbath, from doing thy pleasure on my holy day; and call the Sabbath a delight, the holy of the Lord, honourable; and shalt honour him, not doing thine own ways, nor finding thine own pleasure, nor speaking thine own words: then shalt thou delight thyself in the Lord." Note the two delights: "Call the Sabbath a delight"; "delight thyself in the Lord." The two belong together. We can never find the delight, the special pleasure, in the Sabbath until we see Jesus in the Sabbath, as the Creator that made this world in six days and rested the seventh and blessed it and sanctified it; as the Redeemer who gave up His life and rested during the holy hours of that Sabbath in Joseph's tomb; as the great High Priest who is interceding in our behalf in the sanctuary that the law, with the Sabbath as its seal, may be written in our hearts.

In the chapter in *Desire of Ages* on "The Sabbath," the closing paragraph quotes these verses from Isaiah 58 and then adds, "To all who receive the Sabbath as a sign of Christ's creative and redeeming power it will be a delight. Seeing Christ in it, they delight themselves in Him." The heart of the Sabbath is Jesus, the great Creator, Redeemer.

"O Jesus, let me ever hail Thy presence with the day of rest. Then shall Thy servant never fail to deem Thy Sabbath doubly blessed."

But, dear ones, in order to enter into this double blessing, we need to watch that we do not allow the lax habits of Sunday-keepers to enter into our Sabbath-keeping. As God brings us this holy day from week to week, how many miss the blessing through letting ordinary things come into this extra-ordinary day. "We must be guarded, lest the lax practices that prevail among Sunday-keepers shall be followed by those who profess to observe God's holy rest-day. The line of demarcation is to be made clear and distinct between those who bear the mark of God's kingdom and those who bear the sign of the kingdom of rebellion. Far more sacredness is attached to the Sabbath than is given it by many professed Sabbath-keepers." *Testimonies*, Vol. 6, p. 353.

This chapter in Volume 6 is full of precious suggestions on the observance of the Sabbath. It is worth reading and pondering. The great point is, my dear friends, to accept Jesus as the Creator and Redeemer in the Sabbath; to so love Him and love His truth, that when the great storm comes we shall be so settled in the truth, so sealed in our foreheads with the seal of the living God, that nothing can move us, nothing can shake us.

Dear Lord, write Thy holy law on the tables of our hearts. May we be settled intellectually in knowing Thy Sabbath; may we be settled spiritually in loving Thy Sabbath; and thus may we be among Thy remnant that stand when all the world bows down to the beast and his image. We ask it for the honor of Thy name; for Jesus' sake. Amen.

LIGHT

"For yourselves know perfectly that the day of the Lord so cometh as a thief in the night. For when they shall say, Peace and safety; then sudden destruction cometh upon them, as travail upon a woman with child; and they shall not escape. But ye, brethren, are not in darkness, that that day should overtake you as a thief. Ye are all the children of light." 1 Thess. 5:2-5. It is because we are children of light that we are destined to escape that overwhelming surprise. It is only as we maintain our experience as children of light that we can be saved.

Jesus says, "I am the light of the world: he that followeth me shall not walk in darkness, but shall have the light of life." John 8:12. Since Jesus is the light of the world, all who stay close to Him will remain in the light as the darkness settles down upon this world.

Jesus is in heaven. How does He communicate His light? First, through His law. "The commandment is a lamp; and the *law* is *light.*" Prov. 6:23. So the remnant people of God will be walking in the light of the law. How much of the law? All of it; because James 2:10 says that if we keep the whole law and yet offend in one point, we are guilty of all. You have seen the little colored electric lights on Christmas trees. They are often wired in series; if one goes out, they all go out. So with the Ten Commandments. They are "wired in series," and the only way we get the light and keep the light is to have all the lamps burning. That is one reason why the Sabbath is so important. He who disregards the Sabbath not only loses the blessing of that holy day, but he destroys the authority of all the rest of the law. He has no barrier against sin. Thank God, the remnant church walks in all the light. Every commandment is cherished.

A second channel through which Jesus has chosen to communicate light to His church is spoken of in 2 Peter 1:19: "We have also a more sure word of *prophecy*; whereunto ye do well that ye take heed, as unto a *light* that shineth in a dark place." The reason the law is light is that it is the law of Christ and He is light. And the reason that prophecy is light is that the Spirit of prophecy is the testimony of Jesus. Rev. 19:10.

So, through the law and the testimony, light has been shining down through the ages; and in a special sense, in the days of the remnant, the light will shine beautiful and clear through those two great channels. We find in Rev. 12:17 the summing up of it all: "The dragon was wroth with the woman, and went to make war with the remnant of her seed, which keep the *commandments* of God, and have the *testimony* of Jesus Christ." Praise the Lord, they have the light. They are the children of light. They keep the commandments. They have the testimony.

In Isaiah 8:20, we are given a picture of another situation. How much light is there? No light. "To the law and to the testimony: if they speak not according to this word, it is because there is *no light* in them." I wonder if we really believe that. If we do, we will not be hunting around in the rubbish heaps of Babylon to see if we can discover some brilliant gem. We'll be looking upward to the sanctuary where Jesus, the source of light, is. We will be meditating "in His law" "day and night." David says this brings "delight." Ps. 1:2. And what about the testimonies? "Thy testimonies also are my delight and my counselors." Ps. 119:24. Oh, to fill the mind with all this beautiful light from heaven!

In our last lesson, we noticed the interesting article "Why the Seventh-day Adventists are Succeeding" in the September 1965 issue of *The U.S. Catholic Magazine*. It calls attention to the prominent place the Sabbath occupies in our teaching and practice. The author of this article was not ignorant of the place of the Spirit of Prophecy in the Seventh-day Adventist Church. He says, "Pre-eminent in the SDA movement for nearly 70 years was Mrs. Ellen G. White, who is considered a prophetess by the Adventists. She wrote 53 books and more than 4,500 articles, many of which were based on visions. The role of Mrs. White as a prophetess has disturbed Protestant fundamentalists who would otherwise agree with many Adventist positions such as their literal interpretation of the Bible and sturdy opposition to the theory of evolution." Here we see a clear recognition of the important position of this gift of prophecy in the

Seventh-day Adventist Church. Oh that this gift may fill its rightful place in our experience. We need this light.

In *Testimonies*, Vol. 5, page 667, I read: "It is Satan's special object to prevent *this light* from coming to the people of God, who so greatly need it amid the perils of these last days." Do we need it? Yes, indeed. If it's Satan's special object to prevent this light from coming to the people of God, you can see that he will have special committees busy on this matter. These demons will work in various ways. One of their suggestions is, "Times have changed. Those counsels were all right back there when they were given, but we don't need them now."

Hear Heaven's answer: "Time and trial have not made void the instruction given, but through years of suffering and self-sacrifice have established the truth of the testimony given. The instruction that was given in the early days of the message is to be held as safe instruction to follow in these its closing days." *Selected Messages*, Vol. 1, p. 41. Wouldn't it be strange if Jesus would give light to start us on our journey and then allow the light to be shut off or fade out as we get into the darkest period of human history? Surely the One who gave His life for us will not be thus shortsighted or indifferent. Oh, no! He watches over His church with a tender care and this gift is one of the greatest evidences of His love. These are love letters from the heavenly Bridegroom to His church that is longing for His return. Oh, how blessed we are!

The truth of the matter is, the Spirit of Prophecy, far from being less important, less relevant, less dependable as we near the end, is just the opposite. I read from *Testimonies*, Vol. 5, page 654: "As the end draws near, and the work of giving the last warning to the world extends, it becomes *more important* for those who accept present truth to have a clear understanding of the nature and influence of the *Testimonies*, which God in His providence has linked with the work of the third angel's message from its very rise." So we cannot push these books off to the past. They were a blessing when they were written, but they become much more important as we near the end. But remember, *"It is Satan's special object to prevent this light from coming to the people of God, who so greatly need it amid the perils of these last days." Testimonies*, Vol. 5, p. 667.

He works in various ways. We are told in *Testimonies*, Vol. 5, page 680: "It is not alone those who openly reject the *Testimonies*, or who cherish doubt concerning them, that are on dangerous ground. To disregard light is to reject it." Satan leads some to take their stand against the Spirit of Prophecy; but most of our people acknowledge that God has put this gift in the church. The great danger is in disregarding the light. This is equivalent to rejecting it. You remember the boy that Jesus told about. When his father said, "Son, go work today in my vineyard," he answered, "I go, sir," but he went not. He didn't defy his father. He just didn't go. Oh, how much we need to put into practice the precious counsels that God has given us in these books! Remember, they are all light and "truly the light is sweet." Eccl. 11:7.

On page 681 is a graphic picture of another method the devil uses to keep this light from the people of God. "Many are going *directly contrary* to the light which God has given to His people, *because they do not read the books* which contain the light and knowledge, in cautions, reproofs, and warnings." In order to get the light, we must read the books. Watch how Satan works: "The cares of the world, the love of fashion, the lack of religion, have turned the attention from the light God has so graciously given, while books and periodicals containing error are traveling all over the country. Light so precious, coming from the throne of God, is hid under a bushel."

Suppose I had a bushel basket here, and I would take these books of the Spirit of Prophecy and cover them with the basket. What a strange thing! But this is the danger we are warned against. Someone has pointed out that the bushel is an instrument of commerce, used to measure goods for buying and selling, and that one of the great things that hinders the people of God in their study of these books is the great desire to make money.

"The very last deception of Satan will be to make of none effect the testimony of the Spirit of God. 'Where there is no vision, the people perish.' Satan will work ingeniously, in different ways and through different agencies, to unsettle the confidence of God's remnant people in the true testimony.... There will be a hatred kindled against the testimonies which is satanic." *Selected Messages*, Vol. 1, p. 48. So we see that open oppo-sition, subtle deceptions, cares of this world, are all used by the enemy to keep this light from blessing our lives.

Now, look at a happier picture. Here is a view of the people on whom is shining the accumulated light of the ages, who are "waiting for the coming of our Lord Jesus Christ." Here is a message for us: "I thank my God always on your behalf, for the grace of God which is given you by Jesus Christ; that in every thing ye are enriched by him." (Are Seventh-day Adventists a rich people? Yes, indeed.) "Enriched by him, in all utter-ance, and in all knowledge; even as the testimony of Christ was confirmed in you: so that ye come behind in no gift; waiting for the coming of our Lord Jesus Christ: Who shall also confirm you unto the end, that ye may be blameless in the day of our Lord Jesus Christ." 1 Cor. 1:4-8.

We are rich just in proportion to the degree in which this gift is confirmed in our hearts and lives. You remember we read that the sealing consists in a settling into the truth both intellectually and spiritually so we cannot be moved. We have seen how we are to be settled forever in the matter of the Sabbath and the law. Now we see it is equally important that we be settled, eternally settled, concerning this gift of the Spirit of God, the testimony of Jesus which is the Spirit of prophecy. We noted that it is as we see Christ in the Sabbath that we come to love it and thus are settled in it. So we see that the Spirit of prophecy is the testimony of Jesus. It is His love letter to the remnant church, and as we see Jesus in these testi-monies, we will love this gift and we will become more and more certain of its divine inspiration. Thus it will be confirmed in us.

The Lord wants *every part* of it to be confirmed in us. Think of the *Desire of Ages.* As we study those 800 pages on the life of Jesus and behold our blessed Lord, as we view His life under the magnifying glass, as we see the beautiful details brought out, we are to become "like Him." And thus this gift is confirmed in us.

Concerning *Ministry of Healing* we are told, "This book contains the wisdom of the great Physician." *Testimonies*, Vol. 9, p. 71. As we accept these counsels, they become confirmed in us. We walk in the light on diet and dress, exercise and rest, and proper mental attitudes. We learn by experience the peace, the joy, the health, the life that comes through obedience. Thus we become confirmed. So it is with all the other books. Blessed light, precious light!

Dear Lord, we thank Thee that, in Thy providence, we have been called to be the children of light. As the darkness settles down upon this poor old planet, grant that we shall day by day walk with Thee and teach us how to draw others into this lighted way. For Jesus' sake. Amen.

THE ANCHOR

"Woe to the inhabiters of the earth and of the sea! for the devil is come down unto you, having great wrath, because he knoweth that he hath but a short time.... And the dragon was wroth with the woman, and went to make war with the remnant of her seed, which keep the commandments of God, and have the testimony of Jesus Christ." Rev. 12:12, 17.

The wrath of the devil is sometimes manifested in a roar, in an open attack, but the book of Revelation unmasks also his subtle deceptions. He has many snares, many traps. When a trapper is dealing with an animal that's difficult to catch, he will put a number of traps in different locations around the bait, hoping that in the very effort to avoid one trap, the victim will fall into another. And so it is with the devil. He has many snares, many methods, and he "deceiveth the whole world." Rev. 12:9.

As a part of the ecumenical movement in which papists and so-called Protestants join hands in exalting Sunday, great miracles are to play their part. "He doeth great wonders, so that he maketh fire come down from heaven on the earth in the sight of men, and deceiveth them that dwell on the earth by the means of those miracles which he had power to do in the sight of the beast." Rev. 13:13, 14. So you see that miracles are an important part of the devil's program of deception.

We usually think of the power of spiritualism as we read these verses. Spiritualism is "the spirits of devils working miracles." Rev. 16:14. One of their miracles is to impersonate the dead, but they are not limited to that. The greatest false revival of the ages is just ahead of us, and this will be spiritualism just as truly as the spirits in the séance chamber appearing as the departed dead.

In *Great Controversy*, we have a clear prediction of what's ahead. "The enemy of souls desires to hinder this work; and before the time for such a movement shall come, he will endeavor to prevent it, by introducing a counterfeit. In those churches which he can bring under his deceptive power, he will make it appear that God's special blessing is poured out; there will be manifest what is thought to be great religious interest. Multitudes will exult that God is working marvelously for them, when the work is that of another spirit. Under a religious guise, Satan will seek to extend his influence over the Christian world." *Great Controversy*, p. 464.

So the great counterfeit revival is just ahead. We may even now be entering into it. What will you and I do as it grows in extent and in power? Notice, "Multitudes will exult that God is working marvelously for them, when the work is that of another spirit." Don't forget, this is what takes the whole world captive. This is the ecumenical idea. This draws all the churches together—Catholic, Protestant, and even the world —in a great movement to bring peace and security. But when they have almost succeeded and say, "It is within our grasp," then what about this little group that won't go along? They're the fly in the ointment. They are what's spoiling things. So it is decided to rid the earth of them. Then God will interfere and sudden destruction will come. But before that awful calamity, all the world will have been engulfed in this great religious revival.

Don't think the snare won't be subtle. Don't think it's going to be crude. Jesus says plainly that it will deceive if possible the very elect. Matt. 24:24. So, we need something extraordinary to prepare us. God has given it to us, no question about it. Here it is in the old *Present Truth* of March 1850 (now available in these reprints of the Ellen G. White *Review* articles, Volume 1, page 11): "My dear Brethren and Sisters. This is a very important hour with us. Satan has come down with great power, and we must strive hard, and press our way to the kingdom. We have a mighty foe to contend with; but an Almighty Friend to protect and strengthen us in the conflict. If we are firmly fixed upon the present truth, and have our hope, like an anchor of the soul, cast within the second veil, the various winds of false doctrines and error cannot move us. The excitements and false reformations of this day do not move us, for we know that the Master of the house rose up in 1844, and shut the door of the first apartment of the heavenly tabernacle; and now we certainly expect that they will 'go with their flocks' 'to seek the Lord; but they shall not find Him; He hath withdrawn Himself [within the second veil] from them.' The

Lord has shown me that the power which is with them is a mere human influence, and not the power of God."

This opens up heaven to us, and shows that if our anchor is "within the second veil," then we will not be moved by these false revivals and reformations.

What is up there within the second veil? "The temple of God was opened in heaven, and there was seen in his temple the ark of his testament." Rev. 11:19. The remnant are looking into the most holy place. What do they see there? The ark, the testament, the Ten Commandments. Yes, that's the great center—the law in the ark in the most holy place. And that law is just what this wicked world with all their "religion" does not want. They want to get away from that law, and so Satan is giving them religious tranquillizers of all kinds. But the remnant, instead of drinking the wine of Babylon, are opening their minds to the glory which is shining down from the mercy seat.

Something else is there besides the ark and the law. There's a Man standing at the mercy seat. "Of the things which we have spoken this is the sum: We have such an high priest, who is set on the right hand of the throne of the Majesty in the heavens; a minister of the sanctuary, and of the true tabernacle, which the Lord pitched and not man." Heb. 8:1, 2. Remember that the papacy is the great counterfeit system. It has a priesthood, but it's on earth. It has a sanctuary, but it is on earth. It offers forgiveness of sins, but on earth through a human priesthood. And it has its law, its substitute for God's law in the ark in the temple in heaven. But the remnant are looking upward, their gaze fixed on Jesus in the most holy place. So, they are saved from papal delusions.

"It [the papacy] is prepared for two classes of mankind, embracing nearly the whole world—those who would be saved by their merits, and those who would be saved in their sins. Here is the secret of its power." *Great Controversy*, p. 572.

Let us see how God's message in the sanctuary is the preparation to keep us from yielding to these two ideas.

Consider this matter of "those who would be saved in their sins." How clearly this message shows that if a man is going to find salvation he must come to the sanctuary where that law is. He must meet the law. He must repent. He must give up his transgressions, and put them on the lamb. Then he must come back on the Day of Atonement and join in heart-searching and afflicting the soul and watch outside the sanctuary while the high priest goes in and sprinkles the blood in the most holy place. "For on that day shall the priest make atonement for you, to cleanse you, that ye may be clean from all your sins before the Lord." Lev. 16:30.

The sanctuary service shows that God intends to deliver His people from sin. He is going to get rid of sin, forever. This program that the Church of Rome offers to people of sinning and doing penance, sinning and doing penance, is not the gospel. And the Protestant version of it is not the gospel. Beware of the idea that all there is to the gospel is to be sure to keep your sins confessed. Thank God, there is something more than merely pardon! There is power! The gospel "is the power of God unto salvation to every one that believeth." Romans 1:16.

But watch, if you and I have some darling sins that we would like to hold on to, if we have some weaknesses of the flesh that we would like to excuse, the devil has a snare all ready for us, either in the papacy, or in one of these daughters of the harlot that drink the same wine and echo the same message. We will find something with mighty power that will sweep people off their feet, and we will say, "This is the great power of God; this gives me peace, this gives me release from the conflict. I don't have to fight and struggle any more. All I have to do is simply believe in Jesus and I'll be saved. The Lord knows that I am weak, and so even though I keep on sinning, there'll be a way for me." This subtle deception is what millions believe today.

We have been warned on this point. "No man can cover his soul with the garments of Christ's righteousness while practicing known sins or neglecting known duties. God requires the entire surrender of the heart, before justification can take place; and in order for man to retain justification, there must be continual obedience, through active, living faith that works by love and purifies the soul." *Selected Messages*, Vol. 1, p. 366.

"Let no man present the idea that man has little or nothing to do in the great work of overcoming; for God does nothing for man without his cooperation.... Never leave the impression on the mind that there is little or nothing to do on the part of man; but rather teach man to cooperate with God, that he may be successful in overcoming." *Selected Messages*, Vol. 1, p. 381.

And then this wonderful statement on page 382 that exalts the merits of Jesus and yet makes clear the place of works. The first part of it we often hear quoted; the last part, not so much. We need both. "When it is in the heart to obey God, when efforts are put forth to this end, Jesus accepts this disposition and effort as man's best service, and He makes up for the deficiency with His own divine merit. But He will not accept those who claim to have faith in Him, and yet are disloyal to His Father's commandment. We hear a great deal about faith, but we need to hear a great deal more about works. Many are deceiving their own souls by living an easy-going, accommodating, crossless religion." *Selected Messages*, Vol. 1, p. 382.

Do you see the warning? Babylon today is going pell-mell after this easy religion. All you do is come to the altar, make a decision for Christ, claim that Jesus has accepted you, and go on your way. Don't worry, just have peace. There's a grain of wheat and a bushel of chaff in that, my friends. Oh how we need that view of the most holy place, how much we need to see the ark with the testament in it, and recognize that the judgment is set, the books are opened, and our lives will be measured by that law! How much we need to lay hold of the glorious fact that the plan of salvation contemplates our complete recovery from the power of sin. What a message we have—that the power is there in the most holy place.

But now, on the other hand, notice that statement that the Roman Church is "prepared for...those who would be saved by their merits." Oh what a laborious system of works is in the Roman Catholic ritual! What a mass of ceremony, penance, sack-cloth and ashes, and all the rest! And there is a Protestant counterpart of that. It can creep right into our own midst, into our own hearts—the idea that something we have done or will do can save us. But it is a lie of the enemy. Luther long struggled with that thought. Finally, when the glorious light of justification by faith broke upon his soul, what peace he experienced. It's the thing that burdened Wesley as he sought righteousness. The very word "Methodist" came from their methodical lives. They were seeking, you see, to have everything just right. Read in *Great Controversy* the chapter on "Later English Reformers." See the struggle that Wesley had, and the light that broke upon his soul.

Our very desire to reach the standard of perfection, our very efforts to keep God's law, can lead us into this snare of the enemy to depend upon our merits.

"There are conscientious souls that trust partly to God, and partly to themselves. They do not look to God, to be kept by His power, but depend upon watchfulness against temptation, and the performance of certain duties for acceptance with Him." They must have their prayers every day at a certain time and read so many chapters in the Bible, or they have a guilt complex. That's Romanism, my friends. "There are no victories in this kind of faith. Such persons toil to no purpose; their souls are in continual bondage, and they find no rest until their burdens are laid at the feet of Jesus." *Selected Messages*, Vol. 1, p. 353.

And how is the sanctuary the answer to this problem? We look up there and see not merely a law; we see a mercy seat. We see not merely a standard; we see a great High Priest bearing our nature and the nature of the Deity, lifting His wounded hands and sprinkling the blood upon the mercy seat, and we know that our entrance there is through His name. We know that our victory is through His blood. We do not scale down the standard to meet our poor efforts, but we trust in that all-prevailing Name. Thank the Lord.

The false revivals will not move us as long as our anchor is cast within the veil. Paul speaks of those "who have fled for refuge to lay hold upon the hope set before us." Flee where? "Whither the forerunner is for us entered, even Jesus, made an high priest for ever after the order of Melchisedec." Heb. 6:18, 20. And so instead of imbibing the wine of Babylon, instead of filling our minds with the ideas which are flooding the religious press today, I beseech you, let us turn to Hebrews and Revelation and Leviticus and Daniel. Let us turn to *Great Controversy* and *Early Writings*. Let's fill our minds with the glorious truths of the sanctuary which made and keep us a peculiar people. Let us fix our eyes on Jesus in the most holy place, and we shall be kept from the deceptions which will take the world captive.

Dear Lord, we thank Thee that the temple of God is opened in heaven. As we look, we not only see a holy law which beckons us to perfection, but we see a great High Priest that has given His precious life to bring us to perfection; and we are confident of this very thing, that He which hath begun a good work in us will finish it until the day of Jesus Christ; and we thank Thee in His name. Amen.

THE REMEDY

We come to our last study in this important series on the overwhelming surprise and how we can escape it. "For the grace of God that bringeth salvation hath appeared to all men, teaching us that, denying ungodliness and worldly lusts, we should live soberly, righteously, and godly, in this present world; looking for that blessed hope, and the glorious appearing of the great God and our Saviour Jesus Christ; who gave himself for us, that he might redeem us from all iniquity, and purify unto himself a peculiar people, zealous of good works." Titus 2:11-14.

It is a blessed hope! You notice that the result of it is manifest in the lives of God's children. They are made "a peculiar people." I like some of the other translations: "a people who should be especially His own;" "a people who should be peculiarly His own." As the world is molded more and more by the great enemy, those who are indeed the children of God will be peculiarly His own people.

"A great work is to be accomplished in setting before men the saving truths of the gospel. This is the means ordained by God to stem the tide of moral corruption. This is His means of restoring His mortal image in man. It is His remedy for universal disorganization." *Testimonies*, Vol. 6, p. 11. That's what we need to see—God's remedy. The world has its program to try to cure its ills. The papacy is trying to show men the path of peace. Our nation is trying to demonstrate "the great society" but all these human plans will fail. But God has a remedy. It is the gospel as focused upon this last generation in the three-fold message of Revelation 14.

Notice, "It is His remedy for universal disorganization. It is the power that draws men together in unity. To present these truths is the work of the third angel's message. The Lord designs that the presentation of this message shall be the highest, greatest work carried on in the world at this time." *Ibid.*

Tell me, if the third angel's message is thus appointed by God to accomplish this wonderful purpose, what is my business and what is yours? It is to give this message! "The third angel's message is to be our burden of warning. The side issues are not for us to meddle with." *Testimonies to Ministers*, page 331. And what a multitude of side issues are clamoring for attention from every angle! But the people of God, in the midst of all this confusion, will keep their hearts uplifted, their eyes on the temple in heaven, and their voices sounding the great three-fold message of Revelation 14. Why? Because it's the remedy for universal disorganization. Thank God, His grace "has dawned upon the world with healing for all mankind." Titus 2:11 NEB. All earth's ills—physical, mental, spiritual, political, social, economic—can be cured through accepting the great three-fold message of Revelation 14. This is truly the path to peace. This is truly the way to the great society. There's no other. Are we convinced? Oh, God grant that we may be!

Take this wonderful statement: "In a special sense Seventh-day Adventists have been set in the world as watchmen and light-bearers. To them has been entrusted the last warning for a perishing world. On them is shining wonderful light from the Word of God. They have been given a work of the most solemn import—the proclamation of the first, second, and third angels' messages. There is no other work of so great importance. They are to allow nothing else to absorb their attention. ... They are not to engage in speculation, neither are they to enter into business enterprises with unbelievers; for this would hinder them in their God-given work." *Testimonies*, Vol. 9, p. 19.

What is our work? To give this message. That's what we're here for. That was Noah's work long ago. He was given a message and a work. What would you think if you had found Noah all tied up in business speculation so that he had only a few hours a week to devote to building the ark or preaching the message? What a contradiction, what a travesty. Here is a people appointed to do in our generation what Noah did back there—to give the message that is the answer to the world's problems. We are to allow nothing to divert us.

Again, "The third angel, flying in the midst of heaven, and heralding the commandments of God and the testimony of Jesus, represents our work." *Testimonies*, Vol. 5, p. 383. What's the angel doing? Flying, flying with radio waves; flying through the TV; flying with jet planes; flying with the millions of pages of literature. But ah, friends, remember, even with all those wonderful means of communication, souls are gathered one by one. *It's a sickle that reaps the harvest*, and Jesus is looking for human hands to wield that sickle. He wants us to devote ourselves with undivided attention to living and giving the great message of Revelation 14.

Think of an engine, a battery, some wheels, and other parts. Any use for these things? Very little use for any of them alone, but united, organized they make an automobile which can carry us down the highways. The truths of the great three-fold message of Revelation 14 belong *together*, and it is as we see them together that we discern their full meaning. It is as we present them together that they have power.

Take this matter of the Sabbath. If there's anything that Seventh-day Adventists are known for, it's the Sabbath truth. But now watch, speaking of a certain man who was preaching the Sabbath, but who had not embraced certain other points, "As far as the Sabbath is concerned, he occupies the same position as the Seventh Day Baptists. Separate the Sabbath from the messages, and it loses its power; but when connected with the message of the third angel, a power attends it which convicts unbelievers and infidels, and brings them out with strength to stand, to live, grow, and flourish in the Lord." *Testimonies*, Vol. 1, p. 337.

Where is the power of the Sabbath? It's in connection with the messages of Revelation 14. "*Separate the Sabbath from the messages and it loses its power.*" The message for this hour is not just the seventh-day Sabbath. Think of the Jews that have had the Sabbath for generations. Not long ago I visited a synagogue on Sunday morning to look at the building. They were having their Sunday School classes and their worship services on Sunday! So we see that the knowledge of the Sabbath as a day of rest is not sufficient. It is the Sabbath in the setting of the three-fold message that has the power of God.

The *first message*, "Worship the Creator;" the *second message*: "Babylon is fallen. Come out of her, my people" (the great sign of Babylon is connected with the sun and the sun's day). The *third message* is a specific warning against the mark of the beast, the false Sabbath. The Sabbath stands out in all those three messages. There is the reason for its appeal. There are many people out in the world that know that Saturday is the Bible Sabbath, but they are doing nothing about it. But when they see it in the setting of Revelation 14, a power attends it which convicts unbelievers and even infidels and brings them out to accept this message and walk in the light.

As these issues of creation versus evolution, of the true Sabbath versus the mark of the beast, and of loyalty to God versus loyalty to the papacy, become more and more prominent, it becomes increasingly important to present the Sabbath in the setting of these messages of Revelation 14. That's true with every one of the great pillars of our truth. They support one another. They belong together. They are all parts of the great truth of God.

"The only safety now is to search for the truth as revealed in the Word of God as for hid treasure. The subjects of the Sabbath, the nature of man, and the testimony of Jesus, are the great and important truths to be understood; these will prove as an anchor to hold God's people in these perilous times." *Testimonies*, Vol. 1, p. 300. What three great truths are set forth here? The Sabbath, the nature of man, and the testimony of Jesus—three great truths. These are an anchor to hold the people of God. The Sabbath will hold us against the mark of the beast, which is the sign of the world confederacy in revolt against God. The nature of man will hold us against spiritualism which is the power of the great confederacy. The testimony of Jesus, which is the Spirit of prophecy, is the agency through which the plans of Satan have been unmasked and the plan of God has been revealed. This gift makes us certain that this is the true church. See the anchor, the holding power, in those three great truths? But they belong together as a part of this great threefold message of Revelation 14.

"There are many precious truths contained in the Word of God, but it is 'present truth' that the flock needs now." *Early Writings*, p. 63. Oh, my friends, could it be that even in the study of the Bible men might miss the point? Is it not a fact that when Jesus was on earth, He did not attend the rabbinical schools even though the Old Testament Scriptures were studied? By the time they were 12 years old, the children knew by heart Genesis, Exodus, Leviticus, Numbers, and Deuteronomy. Why didn't Jesus go? Because in the very act of studying the Scriptures, human speculation was so mixed with the Word of God that it was impossible to distinguish between the two, and they did not make a correct application of Old Testament prophecy to the times in which they were living.

So today, there are millions of people in the popular churches studying the Bible; the preachers take their texts from the Scriptures; but oh, there's a message for this hour! "Such subjects as the sanctuary, in connection with the 2300 days, the commandments of God, and the faith of Jesus … establish the faith of the doubting, and give certainty to the glorious future. These, I have frequently seen, were the principal subjects on which the messengers should dwell." *Early Writings*, p. 63.

Here we have the great Advent message; not merely telling that Christ is coming soon, but pointing to the open door in the sanctuary in heaven; showing the law in the ark, the Sabbath in the law, and Jesus as the great Creator-Redeemer that can lift us from sin and make us like Himself; showing that Jesus has sent His angel in these latter days with a revelation through the gift of prophecy; and exposing the designs of Satan in his masterpiece of spiritualism and the papacy. These are the great subjects which, *together*, make a program that God is using to prepare a people for His coming.

I want you to notice how all this is the presentation of Jesus. "There is none other name under heaven given among men, whereby we must be saved." Acts 3:12. But in order to experience the fullness of the saving power of Christ in this last generation, in order to be among these people who walk in all the light as the world goes down in darkness, we need to know Jesus as He has revealed Himself in this message.

Look at your hand—your thumb and the four fingers. I want you to just associate those fingers with these various pillars of truth as they reveal Jesus. Think of that hand as the hand of Christ extended in invitation; think of that thumb as the great truth of His imminent appearing—the coming of Christ. Isn't that good news? "The return of Christ to our world will not be long delayed. Let this be the keynote of every message." *Testimonies*, Vol. 6, p. 406. Tell me, could you present that great truth and leave Jesus out? No.

Now take your index finger. Let this represent the second great pillar—the blessed truth of the sanctuary. And what do we find when we look at the sanctuary? We see a Lamb and a Priest. Who is the Lamb? "Behold the Lamb of God, which taketh away the sin of world." John 1:29. Who is the Priest? "Seeing then that we have a great high priest, that is passed into the heavens, Jesus the Son of God." Heb. 4:14. Can you give the sanctuary message and leave Jesus out? What would you have? Boards and furniture. That's all. Talk about putting Christ in the message! He's there, friends. Just don't leave Him out.

Take the third point, the Sabbath. There you have the seal that makes the people of God different from the world. "Seventh-day Adventists." This is one of the great pillars of this message. Is Jesus in it? Who is the Creator? "By him," Paul says, "were all things created." Col. 1:16. And not only is the Sabbath a sign of creation, but also, "I gave them my Sabbaths, to be a sign between me and them, that they might know that I am the Lord that sanctify them." Eze. 20:12. And who is the Sanctifier? Jesus is. "That great Shepherd of the sheep, through the blood of the everlasting covenant" will "make you perfect in every good work to do His will." Heb. 13:20, 21. Is Jesus in the Sabbath then? Yes, indeed. He's the Creator. He's the Sanctifier. Talk about putting Christ in the message! He is there; and you would have to do a terrible piece of surgery to cut Him out.

Now the fourth point—the testimony of Jesus which is the Spirit of prophecy. We know from Rev. 12:17 that it is one of the great leading truths. Is Jesus in the Spirit of prophecy? What is the Spirit of prophecy? "The testimony of Jesus." Rev 19:10. "I Jesus have sent mine angel to testify unto you these things." Rev. 22:16. This is heaven's great evidence of the love of Christ to the remnant church, the love letters of the Bridegroom to His earthly bride. Yes, Christ is in the message!

Let us look at this last point—the nature of man, the state of the dead. Is our message merely that the dead are unconscious, or is it a message that God has given to us eternal life and this life is in His Son? "He that hath the Son hath life; and he that hath not the Son of God hath not life." 1 John 5:12. Christ as the life giver, the Creator that gave us life in the beginning, the One who maintains our life now, the One who is going to give us immortality at His appearing—Christ is there. Talk about putting Christ in the message! He's there, friends. Oh, don't leave Him out.

And there you have five great landmarks, pillars. Put them together in one, in the great message of Revelation 14, and you have a hand that beckons to heaven, a hand that points the way to the city of God, a hand extended in loving invitation—the hand of Jesus. Oh friends, what else is there to live for, except to give this message? What do you say?

"The grace of God has dawned upon the world with healing for all mankind." And how practical it is. It's not merely a chain of truth, of doctrines. It's a way of life. Take our great work of temperance and health reform. Is it a part of this message? Indeed. The first message says, "Worship the Creator." The human body is His noblest creation. So if we worship Him as Creator, we will want to co-operate with Him in the care of the body.

The second message says, "Don't drink the wine of Babylon." This must include the literal intoxicating potions that are offered to the lips of the people today. It takes a sober people to know and appreciate this message.

The third message presents a people "that keep the commandments of God and the faith of Jesus." And the natural laws are a part of His commandments as well as the spiritual.

Is the out-of-the-cities message a part of the third angel's message? We've been studying the approaching economic pressure of the labor unions and the governments of earth as they combine to enforce the mark of the beast. And what has Jesus told us through His messenger? "Out of the cities is my message." Learn to grow your own fruits and vegetables in preparation for the boycott. You see there is something practical to do as we accept this message.

All the points of truth and practice found in that message of Revelation 14 that make up God's great program for this last hour are practical. And all of it comes from the heart and hand of Jesus.

Dear Lord, we thank Thee for the revelation of Jesus Christ and for the great privilege of sharing with a distraught world the hope of heaven—the message that means life now and life forever more. Help us to prune from our lives and programs every hindering thing. Keep us focused on our job. Help us to carry out our commission and may we share in the glory that is soon to be revealed. For Jesus' sake. Amen.

ENOCH'S OUTPOST

I want to study with you about Enoch, who was translated to heaven without seeing death. So far, two men have gotten out of this world alive—Enoch and Elijah. Will anybody else ever have that experience? Yes, the 144,000 will have that privilege. Think of it, friends! What happened before to only two men is going to happen now to thousands of people. Are any of them around now? We hope so. We remember that stirring appeal from the messenger of the Lord: "Let us strive with all the power that God has given us to be among the hundred and forty-four thousand." E. G. White, *S.D.A. Bible Commentary*, Vol. 7, p. 970. So you and I have a special reason for studying the life and experience of Enoch.

There is not a great deal about Enoch in the Bible; but there is enough so that we can get a picture of his work and experience and apply it to our own. Look at Hebrews 11:5: "By faith Enoch was translated that he should not see death; and was not found, because God had translated him: for before his translation he had this testimony, that he pleased God." Before he was translated, right here in this world, Enoch pleased God and he knew it. That's a wonderful experience, isn't it?

We must have the experience that Enoch had. *Gospel Workers* page 54, after quoting the above text, says: "To such communion God is calling us. As was Enoch's, so must be their holiness of character who shall be redeemed from among men at the Lord's second coming." Will you have an experience like Enoch's? You will, unless you are lost, or unless you die before Jesus comes. Not a one of us wants to be lost; and I'm sure that we cherish the hope of translation. Of course, it is in God's hands whether we rest in the grave or remain alive to be translated; but we are to make translation our goal, our hope, our objective.

Let us notice what the first book of the Bible says about this man. Genesis 5:22-24: "And Enoch walked with God after he begat Methuselah three hundred years, and begat sons and daughters. And all the days of Enoch were three hundred sixty and five years: and Enoch walked with God: and he was not; for God took him." What does it mean, "he was not"? He wasn't here in this world any more; he left it. We're told that people hunted for him, and they couldn't find him: "he was not." Enoch was gone.

Where did he go? He went with God. I've always liked the story the way the little boy told it: Enoch and God used to walk together, and sometimes they'd take long walks together. One day they got so far away from Enoch's home that God said, "Enoch, it's closer to where I live; come on home with Me." Ah, dear ones, such a walk with God! I want to walk with God, don't you?

In *Gospel Workers* page 51, I read: "Enoch's walk with God was not in a trance or a vision, but in all the duties of his daily life. He did not become a hermit, shutting himself entirely from the world." Back in the early ages of Christianity, after the apostasy came in, there were men who had the idea that the way to be holy was to be a hermit—to get off in a cave somewhere and do nothing but read and pray. But Enoch did not become a hermit.

"In the family and in his intercourse with men, as a husband and father, a friend, a citizen, he was the steadfast, unwavering servant of God." So Enoch was a worker, a worker for God; that is how he walked with God.

Was Enoch a preacher? Yes; we're given a view of his preaching in Jude 14, 15: "And Enoch also, the seventh from Adam, prophesied … saying, Behold the Lord cometh with ten thousands of his saints, to execute judgment upon all, and to convince all that are ungodly among them of all their ungodly deeds which they have ungodly committed."

What was Enoch's great subject, according to this? The second coming of Christ. Today he would be called "an Adventist preacher." Away back there his eye was focused upon that grand event, the coming of our Lord with all the angels of glory to reward His saints and execute judgment upon the wicked. No wonder he is set forth as a type for you and me to study—we have the same message to bear that Enoch did!

What do you gather from this verse in Jude, as to the conditions around Enoch? It was an ungodly world. In fact, if you want to get a picture of how wicked it became in Enoch's time, read Genesis 6:5, and you will note that God finally said that the imagination of men's hearts was only evil continually. And the flood had to come upon the world as the consequence.

God is going to destroy the world again. This time, instead of being a deluge of water, it will be a deluge of fire. Is anybody going to get out alive? Yes, the righteous are going to be taken out of this world and preserved, as Noah was preserved. And Enoch's message is as appropriate for this hour as it was back there.

There are two things about Enoch that I want you to notice: First, *separation*. He walked with God; he didn't walk with the world—he walked *in* the world but not *with* the world. Amos 3:3 asks a question: "Can two walk together, except they be agreed?" No, they can't. If you want to go to Chicago and I want to go to New Orleans, we can't travel together. We just have to say good-bye. To walk together, we must be agreed. And the fact that Enoch walked with God is evidence that he *agreed* with God. "Holiness is agreement with God." *Testimonies*, Vol. 5, p. 743. If you and God agree, then you're living the life of holiness. If you don't agree, you don't have holiness. No matter what ecstasy of feeling, no matter how much men shout and sing and pray, if their lives are not in agreement with God, they still do not have holiness.

Before we study this life of holiness that Enoch lived and what he did in order to attain and maintain that life of holiness, let's look at the background. God placed Adam and Eve, our first parents, in the Garden of Eden. He gave them His law; they broke it, and were cast out from the garden and put in this world to learn, by hard toil, the lessons of real repentance and obedience.

I see the tears falling down God's face, as He has to take His children and lead them out of the beautiful garden home, out into a world that must bear the curse of sin. Ah, think of it, friends! Sweat and toil, thorns and briars—these are part of the lesson book in which you and I are to learn how terrible sin is and what a long road it is back to Eden

You remember that Adam and Eve had two sons. Abel was righteous; Cain pretended to be, but he didn't do what God said—he had his own ideas, just like a lot of people today. Cain became so angry because Abel was accepted and he wasn't, that he rose up and smote his brother and slew him. Then Cain fled away from Eden. He went off into another part of the world, and there he built a city (Genesis 4:17). This is the first use of the word "city" in the Bible.

The Lord gave Adam and Eve another son to take Abel's place. As Seth grew up, he was righteous like Abel. He gladdened his parent's hearts by walking in the commandments of God. And his descendants had the glorious privilege of maintaining the truth.

At the head of the two great divisions of mankind stood those two sons of Adam: Cain and Seth. Now I want you to notice something very interesting: "Cain had withdrawn from his father's household. He had first chosen his occupation as a tiller of the soil, and he now founded a city, calling it after the name of his eldest son. He had gone out from the presence of the Lord, cast away the promise of the restored Eden, to seek his possessions and enjoyment in the earth under the curse of sin, thus standing at the head of that great class of men who worship the god of this world." *Patriarchs and Prophets*, page 81.

While Cain was developing his city and those that went with him were developing various arts and sciences, we are told: "Abel had led a pastoral life, dwelling in tents or booths, and the descendants of Seth followed the same course, counting themselves 'strangers and pilgrims on the earth,' seeking a better country, that is, an heavenly.'" *Patriarchs and Prophets*, page 81. Abel dwelt in what? Tents, or booths. What is a booth? Why, it's a house made of vines or trees, an arbor. Is that the kind they had in Eden? Yes, only they were made entirely of living vines or trees. My point is, they were not extravagant, man-made structures in which millions of dollars were piled up. Cain went to his city program, where the works of man were continually exalted; but Seth led out in a pastoral, country life.

"For some time the two classes remained separate. The race of Cain, spreading from the place of their first settlement, dispersed over the plains and valleys where the children of Seth had dwelt." What happened? Why, these Cain-ites moved right in where the Seth-ites had been living! And what did the Seth-ites do? Did they say, "Well, we've got all our investment here, and everything is like we want. It's too bad we have these wicked neighbors around us, with their sinful conversation. Their influence is hard on the children. But there's nothing we can do about it." Is that what they said?

Listen: "The latter [the children of Seth], in order to escape from their contaminating influence, withdrew to the mountains, and there made their home."

If you and I had lived back there and had been under the influence of Seth and had gone along with Seth's program, when the Cain-ites moved in, what would we have done? Moved out and up into the mountains!

"So long as this separation continued, they maintained the worship of God in its purity. But in the lapse of time they ventured, little by little, to mingle with the inhabitants of the valleys." Oh, what a picture! Do you see them? At first they can't bear the thought of the wickedness, the idolatry, the blasphemy, the polygamy, the adultery, the fornication; and they say, "Oh, we must get our children out of here!" and away they go up in the mountains. And for some time they maintain the worship of God in purity up there. But as time goes on, year after year, they ventured to mingle.

And friends, they didn't have radio and television back there. Today, you can have all the influences of Cain right up in the mountains, if you want to spend a few dollars. But back there they could escape. Thank God, we can escape today if we're willing, can't we?

But did you notice, "they ventured, little by little, to mingle with the inhabitants of the valleys. This association was productive of the worst results. 'The sons of God saw the daughters of men that they were fair.' Genesis 6:2. … Many of the worshippers of God were beguiled into sin by the allurements that were now constantly before them, and they lost their peculiar, holy character. Mingling with the depraved, they became like them in spirit and in deeds: … The children of Seth went 'in the way of Cain'; they fixed their minds upon worldly prosperity and enjoyment, and neglected the commandments of the Lord." Do you see the picture, friends? Ah, they got to thinking that they had to have all those things that the descendants of Cain had; and of course, if they were going to have them, they had to get down there into the race with the "sons of men." And so, little by little, many of them became contaminated with that awful influence.

And now, in the midst of the terrible apostasy, Enoch appears. The Spirit of God comes upon him, and his soul is stirred. What does he do? He repeats the experience of Seth; he gets away from those abominations, those idolatrous customs and influences. He cries out, "I can't bear it. I've got to get away from all this; I want to walk with God, and God is not in this sort of thing."

I want to read you something from the Spirit of Prophecy. "He [Enoch] did not make his abode with the wicked. He did not locate in Sodom, thinking to save Sodom." E. G. White, *S.D.A. Bible Commentary*, Vol. 1, p. 1087. Ah, friends, that needs some study! Sometimes we hear this suggestion: "You have to be in the world. After all, how are you going to save them unless you are?" I suppose Enoch heard that argument, but it did not impress him.

"Well," you say, "didn't he do any evangelism?" Oh yes, he was one of the greatest evangelists of antediluvian times! "Well, how does this fit together?" It goes together just right, friends, when we let God put it together. I'm coming to the evangelism; but now I'm studying the separation.

"He placed himself and his family where the atmosphere would be as pure as possible." Personally, I think I need as much help as Enoch needed; in fact, if there's a way to get it, I need more. I don't have the strength of body, or mind, or soul, that Enoch had. Do you? If he needed that help—to get away from the world and its wickedness—friends, I need it! My soul is at stake. I must get ready for translation. And it's going to take something more than coming to the altar in a revival service and saying, "Yes, I believe Jesus died for me and I'm saved no matter what happens." You know I believe in revivals and in the altar call. And people are accepted when they accept Jesus. But, friends, there must be a growth in grace.

Note carefully the following from *Review and Herald*, June 6, 1902: "Are we striving with all our power to attain to the stature of men and women in Christ? Are we seeking for His fullness, ever pressing toward the mark set before us—the perfection of His character? When the Lord's people reach this mark, they will be sealed in their foreheads. Filled with the Spirit, they will be complete in Christ, and the recording angel will declare, 'It is finished.'" That is the experience that those who are translated must have.

Sometimes I hear expressions like this, "It's all very well, I suppose, if you want to go out in the country; but some of us have to be on the firing line, actually working with the world and saving souls." My dear friends, I'm going to come to that—Enoch's method of evangelism—but I say that God has not called any man or his family in these closing hours to lose their own souls in the effort to save others.

What did Enoch do up there? Why did he go there anyway? Without doubt he went up there to be separate from sinners, to get away from their influence; but that's only half of it. The other half is, he went up there to be with God. His errand wasn't accomplished when he got out away from that ungodly influence; he went there to *get* something, not merely to *get away* from something. "Distressed by the increasing wickedness of the ungodly, and fearing that their infidelity might lessen his reverence for God, Enoch avoided constant association with them, and spent much time in solitude, giving himself to meditation and prayer. Thus he waited before the Lord, seeking a clearer knowledge of His will, that he might perform it. To him prayer was as the breath of the soul: he lived in the very atmosphere of heaven." *Patriarchs and Prophets*, p. 85.

Oh, friends, see him as he goes. Is he walking, literally walking? Is that how he got there, from the valley to the mountain? Yes, there was no train or automobile or jet plane. He walked; and he walked with God. I want to take that walk with God, don't you, friends?—a walk that separates me from the sinful influence of this age which is as the antediluvian age for wickedness.

Now I come to the second point: Enoch's evangelism. Enoch, we've already read, wasn't a hermit. He went to the mountain, but he didn't stay on the mountain all the time. If you don't go at all, friends, you may lose your soul in the whirlpool, the cesspool, of the valleys of sin—the cities of iniquity. But if all you do is get back up into the hills and become a hermit, I'm not even sure you'll save your soul; even if you do, friends—shall I put it this way?—you'll be very lonely. God never intended that you should go out and be a hermit with the selfish idea of just saving yourself.

Enoch was a preacher of righteousness. Having entered into an experience with God in the country, he went down into those cities and preached the coming judgments of God on the wicked world and called men to repentance. He received power in the hills with God; and he carried that power down into the cities in the valleys where men lived in prosperity and luxury and vice. There he proclaimed the truth of God in trumpet tones. He was an evangelist!

And now, do you know what Enoch did next? Listen as I read from *S.D.A. Bible Commentary*, Vol. 1, p. 1087: "Enoch did not make his abode with the wicked. He did not locate in Sodom, thinking to save Sodom. He placed himself and his family where the atmosphere would be as pure as possible. Then at times he went forth to the inhabitants of the world with his God-given message. Every visit he made to the world was painful to him. He saw and understood something of the leprosy of sin. After proclaiming his message, he always took back with him to his place of retirement some who had received the warning." Oh friends, when I saw that, I said, "This is it! That's evangelism! That is soul winning!"

And you know, there's a word here that thrills my soul as I look at it: "always." After proclaiming his message, he always took back with him to his place of retirement some who had received the warning. Isn't that wonderful, friends? Yes, he expected to take somebody back. Brother, sister, do you? Is our job merely to warn people? Oh no; it is to get somebody, get hold of them, and get them out!

"Some of these became overcomers, and died before the Flood came." They weren't translated like Enoch; they didn't go through the flood with Noah in the ark; but they were saved. Oh, do you get the picture, friends? I see them. I see Enoch, coming back from his evangelistic trip. He's nearing home now. I see his boys looking down the road. Methuselah, the oldest boy, says, "Daddy's coming, and he's got some folks with him!" And did Enoch's wife and children have things ready? Or do you suppose they said, "Oh my, Daddy is always bringing people home and making more work for us." I don't think so; I think it was understood in that household that their job was to take hold of people, people who needed help to get saved out of that sinful world.

When people have that attitude there's not very much problem in the home of wanting to get down to the cities of sin and have a "good time." No, going to town is not looked upon as a lark; it's looked upon as a mission, and a dangerous mission, like going into a burning building to pull somebody out before the falling wall crushes them; like launching out into the deep to save a drowning man that's already gone down twice. That's what going to these cities is today! God help us sense it! Enoch did.

And so he brings these people home. They are there with him for some time. Day after day they drink in the atmosphere of that home, attend the family worship, eat the meals; and I wonder, friends, if the diet was just the same as what they were used to in the cities? Was it a different diet? You know it was. And do you think that all the popular magazines were lying around for them to read? No. There were a lot of things that were different. And some of the people, as they received that diet for the stomach and that diet for the mind, began to revive. They began to see that this was life! And they said, "Enoch, can't we get into this too?" "Yes," Enoch said, "you can; that's what I pulled you out for." And they persevered, and they were saved. Even though they died, they died in hope; and they'll be resurrected and be in the city of God because Enoch pulled them out to his home in the hills.

"But some had lived so long in the corrupting influence of sin that they could not endure righteousness." Think of it, friends; they couldn't take very much of it. After they'd had it a few hours or a few days, they began to get itchy and fidgety, and said, "Oh, I've got to get back."

And I can hear their excuses. They come around to Enoch, and they say, "Enoch, I appreciate your having me up here, and it's just been wonderful; but there are some things I've got to take care of back in the city." And Enoch knows the symptoms. And oh, friends, it's a pitiful thing. That man goes back down the road, back to the plain. What does he want? He wants a cigarette; he wants a drink of whiskey; he wants some of that bloody meat; he wants some excitement; he wants those races and games; he wants the thrill of fiction; he wants the fornication and adultery that were filling the world at that time; that's what he wants—one or all of those things. And so he goes back to where he can get it, because it isn't up there where Enoch is. He can't endure righteousness. "As a dog returneth to his vomit, so a fool returneth to his folly." Prov. 26:11. Isn't it pitiful? But it must not discourage us; it must lead us to work with all the more earnestness and love.

And remember, friends, some will persevere—some, even of those who seem to be most hopeless, the most degenerate. If we can just get them to quit looking at the things around them, and look to Jesus, on the cross, in the sanctuary, and Jesus in His love revealed in these things of nature.

Oh friends, I'm so glad I don't have to read all that I've been reading to you tonight and simply wish there was something that we could do about it. This day is the scripture fulfilled in your ears.

I want to read you some things from this book, *Evangelism*, pages 76-78: "As God's commandment-keeping people, we must leave the cities. As did Enoch, we must work in the cities but not dwell in them."

"The truth must be spoken, whether men will hear, or whether men will forbear. The cities are filled with temptation. We should plan our work in such a way as to keep our young people as far as possible from this contamination." Shall we take our young people to see the sights and hear the sounds of these cities? Is that the kind of education they need? No, the less they have of that kind of influence, the better.

"The cities are to be worked from outposts." Is that the way Enoch did it? Yes. "Said the messenger of God, 'Shall not the cities be warned? Yes, not by God's people living in them, but by their visiting them, to warn them of what is coming upon the earth.'"

"We must make wise plans to warn the cities, and at the same time live where we can shield our children and ourselves from the contaminating and demoralizing influences so prevalent in these places."

We are told plainly that there should be church buildings in the cities; but our institutions should be outside. "Repeatedly the Lord has instructed us that we are to work the cities from outpost centers. In these cities we are to have houses of worship, as memorials for God." Why? They're life-saving stations; that's what they're for! "But institutions for the publication of our literature, for the healing of the sick, and for the training of workers, are to be established outside the cities. Especially is it important that our youth be shielded from the temptations of city life." God helping us, we want to do it, don't we?

This is the lesson I want to bring to your hearts tonight: Do you see, friends, that it isn't enough to get separated from sin and sinners, and get out in the country? Do you see that it isn't enough just to live in the country and then go out and warn people? What is the next thing to do? Get hold of them and bring them back. Don't misunderstand me; there are some who may be able to be saved where they are. I'm not trying to limit God. But I am showing you plainly from the Word of God and the Testimonies of His Spirit that the only way to save some of these people is to pull them out; and that vision should be in our hearts all the while—looking, looking, like a shepherd looking for his sheep. Jesus is looking: "the eyes of the Lord run to and fro throughout the whole earth." 2 Chronicles 16:9.

What kind of home are you going to bring them to, brother, sister? Do you have a place to bring anybody? What kind of place is it?

Do you remember that when Jesus came back from the wilderness, the Spirit of Inspiration rested upon John the Baptist and he said to his disciples as he saw Jesus coming, "Behold, the Lamb of God!" And Andrew and John followed Him. Knowing that they were following Him, Jesus turned and said, "What seek ye?" They said, "Master, where dwellest Thou?" He said unto them, "Come and see." And thank the Lord, that very hour began a fellowship which never ended.

I ask you again, do you have something to bring people to? All Jesus had, probably, was a little booth down there by the river; that's all. He didn't have any palace. Anywhere God is, and a child of God, is a place for somebody to get close to God.

And that leads us to this point that I want to impress especially: I've asked you what kind of home you have to bring them to; but the vital thing, the very center and core, is this: What kind of experience do you have to share with them? Do you have one? Oh, if you haven't friends, get one! You can; Enoch did, and you can. And don't think it's something you have to wait years for. God longs to do things for people, and at once have them begin to share with others.

Oh friends, let's be so busy getting something from God and sharing it with others that we haven't time for a lot of worryings and complainings, a lot of fears and discouragements, a lot of lusts and ambitions. Let's fill our time and our lives with this one thing. It's like a coin with two faces, and its two faces are these—to get ready for heaven ourselves, and to help get many others ready before Jesus comes.

ADDITIONAL QUOTATIONS

"Who will be warned? We say again, 'Out of the cities.' Do not consider it a great deprivation, that you must go into the hills and mountains, but seek for that retirement where you can be alone with God, to learn His will and way....

"I urge our people to make it their lifework to seek for spirituality. Christ is at the door. This is why I say to our people, 'Do not consider it a privation when you are called to leave the cities and move out into the country places. Here there await rich blessings for those who will grasp them. By beholding the scenes of nature, the works of the Creator, by studying God's handiwork, imperceptibly you will be changed into the same image.'" *Selected Messages*, Vol. 2, pp. 355-356.

"If we place ourselves under objectionable influences, can we expect God to work a miracle to undo the results of our wrong course?—No, indeed. Get out of the cities as soon as possible, and purchase a little piece of land, where you can have a garden, where your children can watch the flowers growing, and learn from them lessons of simplicity and purity." *Selected Messages*, Vol. 2, p. 356.

"It is not God's will that His people shall settle in the cities, where there is constant turmoil and confusion. Their children should be spared this; for the whole system is demoralized by the hurry and rush and noise. The Lord desires His people to move into the country, where they can settle on the land, and raise their own fruits and vegetables, and where their children can be brought in direct contact with the works of God in nature. Take your families away from the cities is my message." *Selected Messages*, Vol. 2, pp. 357-358.

"The Protestant world have set up an idol sabbath in the place where God's Sabbath should be, and they are treading in the footsteps of the Papacy. For this reason I see the necessity of the people of God moving out of the cities into retired country [places], where they may cultivate the land and raise their own produce. Thus they may bring their children up with simple, healthful habits. I see the necessity of making haste to get all things ready for the crisis." *Selected Messages*, Vol. 2, p. 359.

"More and more, as time advances, our people will have to leave the cities. For years we have been instructed that our brethren and sisters, and especially families with children, should plan to leave the cities as the way opens before them to do so. Many will have to labor earnestly to help open the way." *Selected Messages*, Vol. 2, p. 360.

CITIES OF REFUGE

Our text is Amos 5:19: "As if a man did flee from a lion, and a bear met him; or went into the house, and leaned his hand on the wall, and a serpent bit him." What a perplexing picture! Running for his life from a lion, this man runs right into a bear. So he starts running again in a different direction. Finally he sees a house, and says to himself, "Oh, if I could just get into that house, the lion and the bear couldn't get me." So in he goes, and weary, he leans against the wall to rest, and a serpent comes out and bites him. No place to run! No place to hide! Friends, that's the picture of the world today.

Now with this verse, let's put Isaiah 24:17, 18: "Fear, and the pit, and the snare, are upon thee, O inhabitant of the earth. And it shall come to pass, that he who fleeth from the noise of the fear shall fall into the pit, and he that cometh up out of the midst of the pit shall be taken in the snare." What are the people running from? Fear. But as they run from fear, they fall into the pit; and if perchance they get out of the pit, then they are taken in the snare, or trap. Trappers sometimes set several traps, so that as the animal is watching to avoid one trap he backs away and gets caught in another. So today, people are running from one thing and are being caught by something else. But, thank God, in this very hour when people are running from fear, the pit, and the snare, there is a refuge. And how much it is needed. I want to study about that refuge and how you and I can share in it.

When the children of Israel crossed over Jordan and took the land of Canaan, the Lord said to Joshua in Joshua 20:1, 2: "Appoint out for you cities of refuge, whereof I spake unto you by the hand of Moses: That the slayer that killeth any person unawares and unwittingly may flee thither: and they shall be your refuge from the avenger of blood." Anciently, it was a custom that if a man was killed, the nearest male relative took the responsibility for avenging the murder. "The Lord did not see fit to abolish this custom at that time; but He made provision to ensure the safety of those who should take life unintentionally." *Patriarchs and Prophets*, p. 515.

A city of refuge was provided. In fact, there were six of these, three on each side of the Jordan. Among these were such well-known cities as Shechem, Hebron, and Ramoth-Gilead. These were cities of the Levites and priests. It is significant that the very cities in which the ministers of God were located should be selected as places of refuge. This shows how important God considered this work.

Now let's imagine what took place back there. Here is a man out with his neighbor chopping wood, and the ax head flies off and kills his neighbor. But the relatives of the man that has been killed think it was murder, and so they go after the killer. What can he do? My dear friends, there is only one thing to do, and that is to flee, right now. He can't wait to have a farewell party. No, he has to be on his way. Where to? The only place of safety for him is the city of refuge. These cities were located so that they were within a half day's journey of any Israelite's home. The roads had to be kept in good repair at all times. "All the way, sign-posts were to be erected bearing the word 'Refuge' in plain, bold characters, that the fleeing one might not be delayed for a moment." *Patriarchs and Prophets*, p. 515.

Now notice what happened when he came to the gate. The elders were called together to hear the case. If they felt that he deserved protection, what were they to do? "They shall take him into the city unto them and give him a place that he may dwell among them." I wonder if they had a locating committee. Just picture it in your mind. The watchman on the walls looks down the road and reports, "There is a man coming, running fast." He looks again and says, "There's another man running after him." What do they know? They know there is a case coming up. As the first man arrives they give him a hearing, and if he is within the provisions he is taken in and protected. To the avenger they say, "You'll have to go back home for we are protecting this man."

Now the problems begin. Where is he going to live? Who is going to feed him? How is he going to make a living? These are practical problems (and it is interesting what you can read between the lines here when you have some experience in this kind of work). It is very real indeed, for it says, "they shall give him a place that he may dwell among them." The whole series of problems started as soon as that man came in the gate. And they weren't just overnight. You will notice that he had to dwell in that city until the death of the high priest. So they took on some real problems, didn't they? But the Lord said to them, and mind this point, "That is your business. If you live in Hebron or in Shechem or in Gilead, that is your business." What would have happened if when the man came in, the townspeople had said, "I hardly think there is anything around here for you. Things are rather crowded." Should they turn him out, and let the avenger of blood kill him? That would relieve everybody of the burden of solving his problems. You wouldn't have to find a place for him then. Is that the answer, friends? You all say, No! No, indeed. Thank God, we know that part of our work is to be "bothered," to be inconvenienced, so the flee-ing man can find refuge.

Now let's look at what all this represents. First of all, this city of refuge represents Jesus. "God is our refuge and strength." Psalm 46:1. "The name of the Lord is a strong tower; the righteous runneth into it and is safe." Proverbs 18:10. And so we sing with Wesley, "Jesus, lover of my soul, let me to Thy bosom fly.... Other refuge have I none, hangs my helpless soul on thee." Is Jesus our refuge? Yes, each of us may see himself in that fleeing man. Each of us may see Jesus in that city of refuge. Thank God there is a refuge. Aren't you glad? But we had better run and hide in Him.

Yes, Jesus is the city of refuge. But He is not here in this world any more. Has He left anything tangible, something people can see, some-thing to flee to? "The church is God's fortress, His city of refuge, which He holds in a revolted world." *Acts of the Apostles*, p. 11. What is God's city of refuge in this world? The church. There are many organizations in this world that call themselves churches. Could you tell which one is God's city of refuge? Would Revelation 12:17 help you? Yes, God's remnant church is His city of refuge. Do you believe that, friends? If you believe that, where will you be? In the church. If you believe that, what will you try to get other people to do? Get into the church. What for? It is God's city of refuge that He holds in a revolted world.

Now look at this picture: Here is a refugee running as fast as he can for the city of refuge, knowing that the avenger of blood is following hard after him just a mile behind. A man by the side of the road halts him and asks, "Where are you going? Quickly he answers, "To the city of refuge." Then the man by the side of the road says to him, "Let's not be too hasty. There are a lot of rascals up there in that city." But the man's life is at stake. His only safety is in God's city of refuge. Who would try to scare people away from God's city of refuge in this world? Who but the devil? He is the one that is following hard on our track. He wants to destroy us, and we all deserve it. We are his lawful prey. But thank God, there is a refuge in Jesus and in His church. And remember, "Christ and His church are inseparable." "He is the head of the body, the church." Colossians 1:18. Let no one deceive you then with the thought that you can be on good terms with the Head, and yet show no respect to the body. Have you heard the whisper, "Just so you have your name on the church book in heaven, it doesn't make any great difference whether you have it on the church book on earth"? But that suggestion is from the enemy to keep people from getting into the city of refuge. I need a refuge. The avenger of blood is after me. He'd like to kill me. He'd like to ruin my soul for time and eternity. I need a refuge; and what did I read? "The church is God's fortress, His city of refuge which He holds in a revolted world." Well, let's get into the city of refuge and stay there. And let's try to get other people in that need a refuge. What do you say? And let us not join with anybody that wants to wreck the city.

God has within His church various institutions that are to act as soul-saving agencies. Every one of them is to be a city of refuge. For example, I read here in the book *Education*, page 293: "Every school should be a city of refuge." In *Testimonies for the Church*, Vol. 8, page 141, you can read a similar statement about our sanitariums. Yes, God desires every institution to be a city of refuge.

Now I want to ask you something, friends. What is a city of refuge for anyway?—For shelter, for safety from the avenger. What kind of people would you expect to find in the city? I believe if you had gone down the streets back there taking a census you would have found two classes of people. First, refugees—people who were there because they had fled for protection. And you would have found some residents there whose job it was to provide the refuge: to build the houses and keep them up, to maintain the services, the facilities that were necessary for the welfare of the refugees. I wonder how many others were there? Well, I hope there weren't any, friends. When you are using a lifeboat to rescue people from a wrecked ship, there are only two kinds of people that are wanted in that lifeboat—strong men to pull the oars and some people who are being rescued from drowning. Suppose somebody says, "I think I'd enjoy the ride out to the wreck and back. Can I go along, too?" What! You mean that you want to take the seat of a man who could pull the oars? Or take the place of one of those poor drowning souls? "Yes, I'd like to go along for the ride and see the excitement."

I tell you from my heart, friends, there are too many people who want to go along just for the ride in our programs. They don't understand that ours is a work of rescue, not sightseeing. If I seem to be coming too close, then I beg of you to ask God to forgive you for that selfish spirit that has caused you to want to go along just for the ride.

There are two reasons and two reasons only for being in these institutions. If you come as a refugee to get help, our arms are wide open. We are here to help you, and we hope you can get the help you've come for. Now, if you have gotten help, will you join us in providing the facilities and the services that make it possible for us to take in more refugees? If not, will you please make room for others that need help and want it? I speak plainly in order that we may understand the seriousness of this hour. Every time there is a big fire in the city the firemen have trouble with people that just want to watch the excitement. They can't help. They just like to be around our institutions to see what is going on. My dear brother, why not get busy and help us or get out of the way? We have a tremendous job to do, and we need all the help we can get. Souls are dying for physical and spiritual help. Thank God there are cities of refuge; but we need every bed in them. We need every space at the table, day after day, week after week, for two kinds of people—people that *need* help and people that *have* help and are willing to give it to them. Am I putting this too strongly, friends? You wouldn't think so if it were *your* boy or girl that needed to be rescued. If someone had to say, "Sorry, you have run a long way but we can't take you in for we are full and overflowing. We have a number of people that just want to sit by and watch, and so, because of that, we can't take you." Wouldn't that be a tragedy, friends? If it were your boy, your girl, your father, your mother who was fleeing for his life, you wouldn't think that I'm speaking too strongly.

Now God wants not only every church and every institution to be a city of refuge, He wants you personally and your individual home. Did you know your home was to be a city of refuge? Let me read that in *The Ministry of Healing*, page 354: "Our homes should be places of refuge." *Testimonies for the Church*, Volume 6, page 348, says, "If you have a pleasant home invite to it the youth who have no home, those who are in need of help, who long for sympathy and kind words, for respect and courtesy." Isn't that wonderful, friends? This is one of the great reasons for having a home. There are youth that need to be invited; there are the aged, the weary and worn, the sick, the discouraged. There are those that need to learn the message, and to see a demonstration of Christian love. Oh, how many there are that need the sweet influence of a Christian home. Invite them to share the hospitality of your home for a meal, for a day, for a year; for whatever time it takes to rescue them and get them ready for heaven. What a destiny we have! And this is a time of emergency. Oh believe me, the last opportunity to do anything along these lines is just ahead. We could almost measure the time in hours, my friends. Eternity will not be filled with opportunities like this. There will be no cities of refuge in the heavenly Canaan. Everything will be safe from one end to the other; but here and now, danger is all about us. What shall we do about it? Will you make yourself, your home, your institution, your church, truly places of refuge? Will you? Let us respond with all our souls and say, "Yes, thank God, this is my business. I live for nothing else."

We have been talking about refugees fleeing from something. Do they need to? Do you see anything to flee from? You know, the New Testament again and again uses the expression, "the world." 1 John 2:15, 17 says: "Love not the world, neither the things that are in the world. ... The world passeth away and the lust therof. All that is in the world … is not of the Father but is of the world." What is the matter with the world? The devil is at the steering wheel. Jesus called him "the prince of this world." John 14:30. Do you feel like fleeing from this world? Are you trying to get out of this world or do you try to get into it as much as you can? A city of refuge presupposes that somebody needs to flee and wants to flee and get away from something. The world is in league with the devil, but God has His cities of refuge. But they are like islands in a vast ocean of sin and crime and vice. Are you inside? Or are you outside with the world?

You know at the end of the thousand years, at the final judgment, all the righteous are going to be in the city with Jesus. And outside across the great gulf will be the millions and billions and trillions of lost souls, from Cain on down to the last one who lifts his hand against the remnant church. The New Jerusalem will be the great city of refuge. Those who would be inside with Him then must be inside with Him now.

If I understand it rightly, the important thing about this refuge is what is inside and what isn't inside. Inside is sustenance, support, help; outside is the avenger, the adversary, the murderer that would try to destroy your soul. Let's be on the inside, what do you say?

Now I want to ask you some questions; and I pray the Holy Spirit will be very close to us this next little while. If I am a refugee or a Levite, either one, how much of the world do you think I ought to try to drag into the city of refuge? Would it be possible to fill the houses in the city of refuge full of the things that would make it just the opposite of a city of refuge? Has it ever happened? Oh, it has happened so many times that heaven weeps over it.

If the church is God's fortress, His city of refuge, do you think that the residents, whether refugees or Levites, ought to drag heresies into the church? In *Testimonies to Ministers*, page 22, we are told that when men arise, claiming to have a message from God, but instead of warring against the devil and his forces they form a hollow square and turn their weapons upon the church, we are to be afraid of them. "God has not given them any such burden of labor." But I want to tell you something. Our greatest problem is not with these men; our greatest problem is with their sympathizers. It is with people who try to say "good Lord" and "good devil," who try to be friends with all parties, who are too sweet and too Christian to make an enemy. But Jesus made enemies, and so did Paul; and so will you if you stand for truth and right in this crisis hour. Mind you, we shouldn't go out of our way to make enemies. But neither should we go out of our way to keep from doing it. God lays upon you the responsibility of showing that you do not approve the efforts made to destroy the unity of God's church. Don't get involved in a lot of hair-splitting theological arguments. That isn't the problem. The problem is very, very simple and let no one confuse your mind. The question is whether this is God's true church that is going through to the end or whether the church is to be denounced, accused, condemned, and warred against by those who think they have a message from God. How much of that kind of thing do you think we ought to have dragged into the city of refuge, so that when souls come trying to get help they are pulled off to one side and doubts poured into their ears that keep them from getting the help God brought them to receive? How much of that do you think we ought to have, friends? If you will do your duty, we won't have it. When you see things like that, do what the Word of God says: make it a matter of earnest prayer, and then go and reason with the man or woman that dares to drag in those heresies, those criticisms. Plead with their souls, and then if they won't listen to you, take one or two more and carry it through as Matthew 18:15-18 teaches. The camp of God can and must be cleansed. Let's have a city of refuge and not a camp of seduction. What do you say, friends?

Now another point. I was greatly cheered recently when the pastor of the largest church in the Southern Union addressed a letter to all his members dealing with the immodest dress fashions of the present hour. All through the church there are men and women that weep and pray before God in heart burden over the scandalous styles (from head to foot) that are being followed today. The Spirit of Prophecy tells us plainly that the devil invented the fashions, and that fashion is eating out the spirituality of our people and doing more than any other power to separate our people from God. See *Testimonies for the Church*, Volume 4, page 647. I want to ask you a question. When the Lord brings somebody from the world to one of these cities of refuge, do you think he ought to find a refuge? If the fashions of the world today are all right for Christians to follow, why do ministers send out earnest letters to their members, and why do men and women of God in various places all over the land carry a heart burden over these things? Shall we have a city of refuge or shall we have a city of seduction? Shall the young people who come to our cities of refuge look more like the world or less like the world as they linger with us? What do you say, friends? This is something for many to do something about.

Now another point, and it is very practical. Some of the things that people are fleeing from today are alcohol and tobacco. These poisons affect mind and body. Are tobacco and alcohol the only things that have that kind of influence? Why, there are literally thousands of things today that make it difficult for people to get into heaven. And so, in His providence, God has arranged that there shall be cities of refuge where people may come to get away from alcohol, tobacco, and these other things. I ask again, how much do you think ought to be dragged in? If ours are to be cities of refuge, shall they truly be cities of refuge? How much whiskey shall we smuggle in? How many cigarettes shall we make available? Can we get more people in the city of refuge if we have cola drinks in the waiting room? Shall we have a city of refuge or shall we not? What do you say?

The next point will come closer yet to some of us. I want to know, friends, if some distressed and anxious soul comes into a city of refuge how much criticism, faultfinding, and dissatisfaction do you think he ought to hear? Will that help him? Will that be a refuge? I know that some of you hear criticism from people who come and go. Let us ask two questions: First, have they ever gone out and demonstrated how to carry on an institution that is a city of refuge and make a success of it? Next, do they think of any place that is doing the kind of job they think ought to be done? If they do, where should they be? They ought to be there helping to make it succeed; do you agree? They ought to be out with a lifeboat getting people and bringing them in. And may I add, don't be flattered when a visitor begins to tell you the faults of some other place. Remember it is only a matter of weeks or maybe hours until they are off to some other part of the world telling about the faults of you and your place. Don't be deceived; and don't join in the cannibalism. Let's have a city of refuge where poor, tempest-tossed souls can come and find peace and rest and not be harassed with dissatisfaction, murmurings, and criticism.

Our business as Levites is to be sure that ours are cities of refuge. A current idea is that if we could get the furniture expensive enough, and the facilities elaborate enough, and everything comfortable enough that we would have a much better city of refuge. We are warned about this in *Medical Ministry*, page 167. "Those who are influenced against the truth by a lack of extravagance in house, in furniture, in dress, in equipage, show that they are incapable of understanding the merit of truth. ... God is dishonored when those connected with the work which is to prepare a people to stand the test of the time of trouble before us, forsake Him to follow the fashions of the world. ... You are not to seek that popularity which has led far away from the simplicity of Christ. ... Those who believe the truth will never be ashamed of the gospel of Jesus Christ. The principles of truth are to pervade our medical institutions. And then, as those who have followed the customs and fashions of the world shall in their suffering come to these institutions, they will see a simplicity that will charm their senses. They will feel the unseen presence of heavenly angels." Friends, I want that, don't you? Many of these refugees are fleeing the complexity, the luxury, and the heart burdens that the things of this world are causing. They are looking for a quiet place in the hills like Enoch had. And that's not Fifth Avenue brought to the mountains, either.

Now may I ask you this? If somebody wants to drag in these things that I have put the finger on, or other like things that might be mentioned, whose money do you think they should use to do it? Is it fair to take the facilities that have been provided by the money, the sweat, the tears, and the blood of those who believe in these principles of reform, and use those facilities to go exactly the opposite direction? Is it? No. A thousand times, no. The world is wide, and I submit that the honest thing for the man to do—the man who thinks that the way to run a city of refuge is to drag in these worldly things—is to go out and find a place and finance it with his own money or the money of those who agree with his theory. And let those who believe that God wants a place free from all these things continue to carry out a program where those who want that absence of the world can find it. What do you say? Oh, the Lord grant it, my friends.

And now I appeal to your heart: let no one sit in judgment on his brother. But go to your knees and ask God what this means to you. Ask Him what it means to have a city of refuge in a world that is almost all gone over to the devil. Ask Him what it means to have a place—your home, your institution, your church—that is like a boat in the water. Surrounded with the billows of this world, the church is safe if we do not allow the water to get in the ship.

In closing, let us think again of the two kinds of people in the city: the people who come for refuge and the people that are there to help them find refuge. Will you ask God to make your home a place where people can find refuge from sin, refuge from the world, a little bit of heaven to go to heaven in? Let us plead with God and one another until every bit of heresy, every bit of worldliness, every bit of criticism, is banished from our hearts and homes. Remember that to establish this city of refuge—His church and every agency of it—Jesus gave His own life. That we might be free from the avenger of blood, Christ took the stroke upon Himself. I am so glad that the One who died for us lives for us, and that it is His hand that beckons to the gate of refuge. It is His arm that reaches out to draw the refugees in to safety. May God grant that each of us may become a part of the great life-saving team that welcomes men and women and youth who need a refuge, and that these institutions may be used in the great medical missionary program "to make ready a people prepared for the Lord."

MEDICAL MISSIONARY WORK

"Study Christ's definition of a true missionary: 'Whosoever will come after Me, let him deny himself, and take up his cross, and follow Me.' Mark 8:34. Following Christ, as spoken of in these words, is not a pretense, a farce. Jesus expects His disciples to follow closely in His footsteps, enduring what He endured, suffering what He suffered, overcoming as He overcame. He is anxiously waiting to see His professed followers revealing the spirit of self-sacrifice.

"Those who receive Christ as a personal Savior, choosing to be partakers of His suffering, to live His life of self-denial, to endure shame for His sake, will understand what it means to be a genuine medical missionary." *Counsels on Health*, p. 511.

"Medical missionary work is yet in its infancy. The meaning of genuine medical missionary work is known by but few. Why? Because the Savior's plan of work has not been followed." *A Call to Medical Evangelism*, p. 11.

What is "genuine medical missionary work"? Who is "a genuine medical missionary"?

There are many movements in the world today seeking to benefit humanity. We may be sympathetic with their objectives and do what we can to encourage them in their good work. But God has given to Seventh-day Adventists a program of life and health for body and soul which occupies a unique place.

"True medical missionary work is of heavenly origin. It was not originated by any person who lives." *Medical Ministry*, p. 24.

With due recognition of the great work that has been done by such noble spirits as Pasteur, Trudeau, Florence Nightingale, and Clara Barton, it is not to them that we look as the originators or the exponents of the program of medical ministry which has been committed to us. Our health message is as distinctive as our doctrinal message.

Let us examine "medical missionary work" in the light of three great principles. Perhaps we can think of them as three sieves. Some things can pass one test, some may stand two. But only that which passes all three is "genuine medical missionary work."

SIEVE NO. 1: MOTIVE

The true medical missionary is moved by the spirit of loving service (not by professional pride or the desire for money). "Genuine medical missionary work" is sacrificial. Study again the heart-searching words quoted in our opening paragraphs. Christ, the great Medical Missionary, has left us an example. Who will follow in His steps, ministering in His name, not for money, but for love's sake?

True, the financial part of medical missionary work must be conducted in a business-like way. God has given precious instruction on this phase of the subject. But none of this alters the fact that love—true, unselfish love—must be the *motive* of all our work. "And love will be revealed in sacrifice." *Christ's Object Lessons*, p. 49.

These principles can be manifested by an institution only as they fill the hearts of individual workers. Let us each ask the question, "Am I 'a genuine medical missionary'? Have I accepted the Savior's call to share with Him His life of sacrificial service, not for money, not for fame—just for love?"

It is not our purpose here to criticize men and women of the world, to whom the care of the sick may be merely a profession and means of making money. We are pointing out that this is not "genuine medical missionary work." It is not following the example of Jesus. It does not pass through the first sieve. "We are not to cover mercy with selfishness and then call it medical missionary work." *Medical Ministry*, p. 31.

What a pity that the very agency God gave us to be a revelation of His self-sacrificing love, should become one of the greatest money-making activities! How have the sacred pipes, dedicated to the one task of conveying the golden oil of love from the heavenly sanctuary, been prostituted to the service of self! "Some follow worldly policy in order to accumulate means, as they say, for God's service. But God does not accept such offerings. He says, 'I hate robbery for burnt offering.'" *Medical Ministry*, p. 125.

"All heaven is looking on with intense interest to see what stamp medical missionary work will assume under the supervision of human beings. Will men make merchandise of God's ordained plan for reaching the dark parts of the earth with a manifestation of His benevolence?" *Medical Ministry*, p. 131. Study also pp. 124, 125.

Sieve No. 2: Method

The medical missionary is deeply interested in the relief of human suffering. But he is still more concerned with the task of bringing human lives into harmony with the laws of nature, which he recognizes to be the laws of God as truly divine as the Ten Commandments. Therefore, while he uses the simple remedies the Lord has provided to relieve pain, he seeks to lead the mind of the sufferer to an appreciation of God's way of life and the blessings of obedience. And he cannot be satisfied merely with the abatement of unfavorable symptoms.

Jesus' answer to the tempter shows that it is better to suffer as a result of obedience, if providence so orders, than to be free from suffering in transgression. Therefore, *education, leading to obedience, is more important than any apparent results.*

The medical missionary is a teacher, giving instruction in the principles of healthful living, using "a knowledge of physiology and hygiene" as "the basis of all educational effort" *Education*, p. 195.

As in the first great principle, so here, Christ is our Example. "When Christ healed disease, He warned many of the afflicted ones, 'Sin no more, lest a worse thing come unto thee.' Thus He taught that they had brought disease upon themselves by transgressing the laws of God, and the health could be preserved only by obedience." *Ministry of Healing*, p. 113.

"Teach the people that it is better to know how to keep well then how to cure disease. Our physicians should be wise educators, warning all against self-indulgence, and showing that abstinence from the things God has prohibited is the only way to prevent ruin of body and mind." *Testimonies*, Vol. 9, p. 161.

The people "need to be taught that every practice which destroys the physical, mental, or spiritual energies is sin, and that health is to be secured through obedience to the laws that God has established for the good of all mankind." *Ministry of Healing,* p. 113.

If obedience, based on knowledge of nature's laws, is more important than relief of symptoms, what shall we say of any method which promises to cure disease or relieve pain without teaching obedience? What master mind inspires the effort to persuade men and women that they may eat as they please, or disregard God's laws in other ways, and still find a means of healing *without learning and obeying* the laws of health?

Is not this inherent in the false miracles of healing, which we know will increase as we enter the final conflict? Is not this the basic error in drug therapy, making it even more damaging to the soul than to the body? And is not this danger present in many "drugless" methods?

Even in the use of the Lord's appointed remedies, we need to remember that education, leading to obedience, is most important.

SIEVE NO. 3: GOAL

The true medical missionary cannot be satisfied with ministering only to the body. In fact, his primary burden, never forgotten, is for the eternal salvation of those for whom he labors.

And is this not most reasonable? For, if love leads him to give of his best, that physical health may be restored and a patient's life be extended a few years, will not the same love lead him to make most earnest efforts to extend that same life through eternal ages?

How can I say I love a man so much that I will try to save his life for this world, and yet be indifferent to the opportunity to save his life for the future world?

Soul-winning, then, is the *goal* of all true medical missionary work. "We should ever remember that the object of the medical missionary work is to point sin-sick men and women to the Man of Calvary, who taketh away the sin of the world." *Ministry of Healing,* p. 144.

And once more, the Savior appears as our great Example: "Jesus *was not satisfied* to attract attention Himself merely as a wonderworker or healer of physical disease. He was seeking to draw men to Him as their Savior." *Ministry of Healing*, p. 31.

Years ago, the Spirit of Prophecy pointed out the danger of losing sight of this great objective in one phase of our medical missionary work. As we read this quotation, let us remember that this principle applies to every other phase. "There is danger of the workers losing sight of the work of soul saving as they carry forward the business part of the enterprise. There is danger that the business part of the work will be allowed to crowd out the spiritual part.

"Some good is being done by the restaurant work. Men and women are being educated to dispense with meat and other injurious articles of diet. But who are being fed with the bread of life? Is the purpose of God being fulfilled if in this work there are no conversions? It is time that we called a halt, lest we spend our energies in the establishment of a work that does little to make ready a people for the coming of the Lord.

"The only object in the establishment of restaurants was to remove prejudice from the minds of men and women, and win them to the truth. It is not the large number of meals served that brings glory to God. What does this avail if not one soul has been converted, to gladden the hearts of the workers? . . . Unless our restaurant work brings favorable spiritual results, let the world do their own serving of tables and let the Lord's people take up a work in which their talents will be put out to the exchangers." *Medical Ministry*, pp. 306, 307.

We repeat, this principle applies not only to health restaurants, but to every other phase of our medical missionary work. Surely we cannot be satisfied unless, through our efforts, souls are being won to Christ and His message.

Now, with hearts uplifted to God in prayer for His Spirit's conviction, let us examine whatever we are doing which we have called medical missionary work. And let us not seek to judge others. Rather, "let a man examine himself."

1. Is my work done wholly from love—unselfish, self-sacrificing love?

2. Am I more concerned with leading people to obedience to nature's laws than I am to relieving symptoms? And are the methods I am using accomplishing that result?

3. Is my great goal in all my work the winning of souls for Christ and His message? And is the program I am following, the work I am doing, producing souls that I can present to Jesus at His coming?

LEFT, RIGHT, OR CENTER

❧

"And therefore will the Lord wait, that He may be gracious unto you, and therefore will He be exalted, that He may have mercy upon you: for the Lord is a God of judgment: *blessed are all they that wait for Him.*"

"And thine ears shall hear a word behind you saying, This is the way, walk ye in it, when ye turn to the right hand and when ye turn to the left." Isaiah 30:18, 21.

There is a blessing for those who wait. But there are those who don't seem to be able to wait. They get into difficulty as Saul did. He waited seven days for Samuel, and when the time passed and Samuel had not appeared, he said, "I forced myself therefore, and offered a burnt offering." Something *had* to be done! But Samuel said, "Thou hast done foolishly." 1 Samuel 13:12, 13.

Great blessings are ahead for those who can wait for the Master.

Now, note the wonderful promise: When we are in danger of turning to the right hand or to the left, in danger of "swerving," we will hear a voice—*His* voice—say, "Don't do that. Keep in the path."

"And when you swerve to the right or left, you hear a voice behind you whispering, 'This is the way, walk here.'" Isaiah 30:21. [1]

Early in His dealing with His people, God admonished them to stay on the narrow road and beware of swerving. "Ye shall observe to do therefore as the Lord your God hath commanded you: ye shall not turn aside to the right hand or to the left." Deuteronomy 5:32.

"God calls for men and women of stability, of firm purpose, who can be relied upon in seasons of danger and trial, who are as firmly rooted and grounded in the truth as the eternal hills, *who cannot be swayed to the right or to the left.*" *Testimonies*, Vol. 4, p. 75.

---

[1] From *The Bible: A New Translation* by James Moffatt. By permission of Harper & Row Publishers, Inc.

What is the reason for such admonitions? Are the people of the straight and narrow road so prone to get off on one side or the other? "There is in human nature a tendency to run to extremes, and from one extreme to another entirely opposite." *Testimonies*, Vol. 5, p. 305.

If you really are in the middle of the road, you may be challenged from both sides. Those to the extreme right, in deploring the extreme left, often identify the center with it; and vice versa. So don't become confused if you are shot at from both sides. Those who will finally triumph with the advent movement will be those "of firm purpose" who can discern and avoid any divergence, either left or right. Determined to hold solidly with the center, the hard core of loyalty to God's remnant church, they refuse to be turned aside, either by their own tendencies or by the lure of popular deviations.

On one side are the compromisers. It matters not whether we think of them as off on the right or the left, they are off. But they are the very ones who confidently boast that they are in the middle of the road. Jesus told about a broad road that *many* choose, and stated plainly where that road leads. Could it be the compromisers are in the middle of *that* road? It is the one that has room for all the various kinds and shades of compromise.

How can we recognize the compromisers? For one thing, they lean toward the world. When any question of standards comes up, they are found on the worldly side. If you are at all affected by this very human tendency, beware. Be afraid of it.

The compromisers say that "times have changed," (see *Testimonies for the Church*, Vol. 5, p. 211), and so much that is in the Spirit of Prophecy writings does not apply now. Thus they find themselves following their own leading, which results in going along with the crowd. Let us examine ourselves!

The compromisers think it is only the fanatical alarmists who deplore compromise, but they are mistaken. Elder C.H. Watson, while he was president of the General Conference, wrote: "There is setting in on this people a tide of worldliness to which we are surrendering. I do not mean to imply that we are not resisting these influences at all; but I believe that the measure of resistance that we are putting forth is not holding us. We are gradually being swept backward, and should be alarmed about it.... Our resistance of worldly influences is seriously diminishing. I am troubled by the direction that our educational and training work is definitely taking. I am concerned by the more and more obvious fact that in the education and training of our workers we are inquiring more of the world and less of God than formerly."—*Review and Herald*, Nov. 21, 1935.

Elder J.L. McElhany, following Elder Watson as president, on more than one occassion gave expression to his deep concern over the worldly trends within the church. Notice this statement: "Our greatest danger today is the attitude taken by so many of our people of accepting with apparent satisfaction their present low spiritual condition, and not being very much concerned about it.... 'The time has come for a thorough reformation to take place.' ... There has come into the church a listlessness, a carelessness that is deplorable."—*Review and Herald*, Dec. 3, 1936.

In the *Review and Herald* of March 11, 1965, Elder Ernest Lloyd writes under the heading, "Let Us Be True to God's Standards": "In a Methodist church paper appeared the following: 'The Seventh-day Adventist people, like the early Methodists, were plain and humble in life and teachings, but, alas, we have *all* drifted away from the early standards, and our spiritual strength is decayed.' It is conformity to the ways of the world that has brought the spiritual decay. We *must* return to the standards if we are to meet God's expectations for us."

Such appeals should help us to realize that now is the time for God's people to be concerned about the road they are traveling—to be turning *from* the world, instead of *toward* it.

Another characteristic of the compromisers is that they tend to accept human reason above the revealed wisdom of God. "There is a spirit of idolatrous exaltation of mere human reason above the revealed wisdom of God.

"There are men among us in responsible positions who hold that the opinions of a few conceited philosophers, so called, are more to be trusted than the truth of the Bible, or the testimonies of the Holy Spirit." *Testimonies*, Vol. 5, p. 79.

The compromisers also excuse and defend compromise on the grounds that it is supposed to increase the influence of the truth. Does it? "We are not to elevate our standard just a little above the world's standard; but we are to make the distinction decidedly apparent. The reason we have had so little influence upon unbelieving relatives and associates, is that there has been so little decided difference between our practices and those of the world." *Testimonies*, Vol. 6, pp. 146, 147.

The compromisers deplore the supposed disloyalty of those who will not unite with them in tending toward the world. And while talking of loyalty to the denomination, they at the same time lend their influence in direct opposition to the high standards set forth in official actions of the General Conference. When they see an endeavor to uphold these high standards, they may take alarm at the supposed innovations. They think something new and strange is being brought in. They seem to be unaware that these standards are the same that always have been upheld by the Bible and the Spirit of Prophecy, and by repeated appeals from the leadership of the church.

The high standards are none other than "the faith which was once delivered unto the saints." Let us not be deceived by the "loyalty" that frowns upon efforts to live and teach the standards of the church. Such so-called loyalty is treacherous. The treachery of it is set forth in the following inspired passage: "The time is not far distant when the test will come to every soul. The mark of the beast will be urged upon us. *Those who have step by step yielded to worldly demands and conformed to worldly customs will not find it a hard matter to yield to the powers that be*, rather than subject themselves to derision, insult, threatened imprisonment, and death.... In this time the gold will be separated from the dross in the church.... Many a star that we have admired for its brilliancy will then go out in darkness. Chaff like a cloud will be borne away on the wind, even from places where we see only floors of rich wheat." *Testimonies*, Vol. 5, p. 81.

Notice that when the mark of the beast is enforced, the compromisers will go out. But where will they be until that time? In the church, exerting their world-loving influence. Should we have the kind of supposed loyalty that goes along with such an influence because it is prevalent? Decidedly not! On the other hand, should we because of its prevalance, condemn the church? Never! Be true to the church; it is God's remnant people, though faulty. Resist compromise. The time is near when compromisers will go out. Refuse to follow those who do evil, though they be a multitude. Follow the Voice that guides in the narrow way, saying, "This is the way, walk here," though it may seem at times a lonely road.

On the opposite side from the compromisers are the spurious reformers—the critics. They display a lack of confidence in the leadership of the church, and will not submit to organization. There are various degrees of this error, but the least manifestation of it is characteristic and is to be shunned. The inspired writings are clear on this also: "It is hardly possible for men to offer a greater insult to God than to despise and reject the instrumentalities that He has appointed to lead them." *Testimonies*, Vol. 3, p. 355.

The criticizers seem to be imbued with the idea, supposedly from their understanding of the *Testimonies*, that God will bypass the movement to use a few scattered critics. What do the *Testimonies* say about this? "There are little companies continually arising who believe that God is only with the very few, the very scattered, and their influence is to *tear down and scatter* that which God's servants build up." *Testimonies*, Vol. 1, p. 417.

This is not God's way, for just before this, it says: "God is bringing out a people and preparing them to stand as one, united, to speak the same things, and thus carry out the prayer of Christ for His disciples."—*Ibid.*

The criticizers imply that a new movement is necessary. Some actually split off to start a new one. We have had these all along the way for the last 100 years. Some of them, while participating in offshoot-ism, have emphatically denied any such intentions.

It is a subtle variation of this theme to profess confidence in the movement, but imply a lack of confidence in its leadership. How does God regard such an attitude? Listen: "You will take passages in the *Testimonies* that speak of the close of probation, of the shaking among God's people, and you will talk of a coming out from this people of a purer, holier people that will arise. Now all this pleases the enemy. We should not needlessly take a course that will make differences or create dissension. We should not give the impression that if our particular ideas are not followed, it is because the ministers are lacking in comprehension and in faith, and are walking in darkness." *Selected Messages*, Vol. 1, p. 179.

Korah, Dathan, and Abiram lost confidence in God's ability to lead through His chosen human agents. They demanded a change of leadership. But they found out how God regards such an attitude. (See Numbers 16.) Beware of those who quote the *Testimonies* to support their expressed or implied representations that this movement must have a change of leadership. What if mistakes have been made? Does that justify becoming Korahs, Dathans, and Abirams? Why didn't God preserve such men to bring about a reform in ancient Israel?

When God chooses men to deal with errors among His people, He desires them to go about this work in the right way, and the right way does not include circulating reports that are derogatory to the church and its leaders. But this is the very thing the criticizers do. When a leader makes a mistake, they pounce upon it like a buzzard on a corpse, and call all the other buzzards to come and enjoy it with them. If we love the church as Jesus loves it, we will not be eager to promote reports that reflect on the church and its leadership, or even listen to them.

But what if the reports are true? Have we any inspired counsel here? Listen: "Elder _____, you have undertaken to point out the defects of reformers and pioneers in the cause of God. No one should trace the lines which you have done. You have made public the errors and defects of the people of God, and in so doing have dishonored God and Jesus Christ. I would not for my right arm, have given to the world that which you have written. You have not been conscious of what would be the influence of your work." Ellen G. White, *Letter* 48, 1894, in "Elmshaven" Group "M."

But doesn't the Bible tell about the mistakes of God's people, even the leaders? Yes, but does that give us license to do the same? "Let God by inspiration trace the errors of His people for their instruction and admonition; but *let not finite lips or pens* dwell upon those features of the experience of God's people that will have a tendency to confuse and cloud the mind."—*Ibid.*

The fact that God tells the mistakes of Moses, David, Peter, and others should not lead us to think we are to give publicity to what we see as errors and mistakes of our brethren. God knows when to publish mistakes and how to do it. But is it not presumptuous in mortal man to put himself in the place of God? Magnifying mistakes helps nobody. It only multiplies the error and the guilt. "God will charge those who unwisely expose the mistakes of their brethren with sin of far greater magnitude than He will charge the one who makes the misstep."—*Ibid.*

So when we hear of a mistake, shall we ascertain what is the matter and then publish it? Not if we are followers of Christ. Those who are anxious to follow His voice will not be eager to spread reports, even though true, that will multiply the influence of the mistake and create lack of confidence. To do so is to work, not with Christ, but against Him.

"Criticism and condemnation of the brethren are counted as criticism and condemnation of Christ."—*Ibid.*

Furthermore, to circulate true reports of mistakes is to place ourselves where we are apt to fall into dealing in erroneous reports. Elder and Sister White suffered keenly through the circulation of false reports by some of the brethren whose love and confidence they deserved and should have had. Sad to say, the inclination to deal in evil reports has not yet been eradicated from the church. What is the basis of such an inclination, and where does it lead? "There is a class ... who profess to believe the truth, but who cherish *secret feelings of dissatisfaction* against those who bear the burden in this work.... Such readily receive, cherish, and circulate reports which have no foundation in truth, to destroy the influence of those who are engaged in this work. *All who wish to draw off* from the body will have opportunity. Something will arise to test everyone. The great sifting time is just before us. The jealous and the faultfinding, who are watching for evil, will be *shaken out.*" *Testimonies*, Vol. 1, p. 251.

Now I bring you a happier picture—the center. They are not the compromisers and they are not the criticizers. They WILL NOT *compromise* and they WILL NOT *criticize*—that is it in a nutshell, friends! They "will not hold their peace to obtain favor of any." *Testimonies*, Vol. 5, p. 210. They speak out against sin—not by accusing the church and its leadership, but by dealing with great principles of truth that God has given His people and presenting the inspired counsels that lead heavenward.

Those who are in the center, and have swerved neither to the right nor to the left, are very careful not to urge their personal views so as to create division. This distinguishes them from both criticizers and compromisers. "The Word of God does not give license for one man to set up his *judgment* in *opposition* to the judgment of the church, neither is he allowed to *urge his opinions* against the opinions of the church." *Testimonies*, Vol. 3, p. 428.

If we listen to His voice the Lord will teach us to be humble and to use restraint upon ourselves. James White had occasion to exercise such self-restraint. There were some things he believed concerning the prophecies that his wife, as the messenger of the Lord, admonished him to keep still about, even if right. Jones and Waggoner, when the Lord was using them in the 1888 message, were likewise counselled against teaching certain things because they would create division. (See *Counsels to Writers and Editors*, pp. 75-82).

Those who are in the center, though humble and harmless, are to form the hard core of the church militant, unshaken and unshakable. God is counting on them for the great final demonstration. They will not compromise, as did Judas. Neither will they cut off ears, as did Peter. They have no use for the sword of criticism, but humbly "follow the Lamb whithersoever He goeth." They will weep with Him in Gethsemane and suffer with Him in the judgment hall. Never will they swerve from Him to compromise or to criticize. Their hearts are burdened for Israel. They are pictured in Ezekiel 9, which has its application today in the closing hours of human probation. Men with slaughter weapons are standing, waiting for the word to slay.

But just before the slaughter there is a work of marking, or sealing, that goes on. In the fourth verse, the Lord says to the man with the writer's inkhorn: "Go through the midst of the city, through the midst of Jerusalem, and set a mark upon the foreheads of the men that sigh and that cry for all the abominations that be done in the midst thereof." This is God's way of dealing with the present situation, both with the compromisers on the one hand and the criticizers on the other. Everyone who is heart to heart with Jesus will sigh and cry, joining Him at the Mercy Seat in earnest intercession. Are you spending time in this supplication? The angel is coming from door to door; he is listening. Is there somebody praying, somebody weeping—praying and weeping for the compromising and the criticizing? Oh! this is enough to pray for and weep about.

Just ahead is the last conflict of the church. It is going to mean everything, friends, to be a part of that center core of the church that is unshaken and unshakable. It is strong to resist the tide of worldliness; it is equally strong to resist the spirit of criticism. It is determined to help answer the prayer of Christ that His church "may be one" as He and the Father are one. Shall we have a part in this? If we do, we shall bring joy to the heart of God and to all our true leaders who, with Jesus, are longing to see a people that reflect fully the divine image.

THE CHURCH OUR MOTHER

❖⟫⟨❈⟫⟨❖⟫⟨❈⟫⟨❖

L et us repeat together Revelation 12:17: "And the dragon was wroth with the woman, and went to make war with the remnant of her seed, which keep the commandments of God, and have the testimony of Jesus Christ."

The dragon is Satan. Revelation 12:9. The woman is the church. Ephesians 5:23. The devil is angry with the church and goes to make war with the remnant—the last—of her seed. And what does the seed mean?—Children. The Lord told Abraham that his seed, children, would be as the stars of heaven. Genesis 15:5.

Commenting on our text, the Spirit of Prophecy says: "The people of God, symbolized by a holy woman and her children, are greatly in the minority. In the last days only a remnant exists. John speaks of them as those that 'keep the commandments of God and have the testimony of Jesus Christ.'" *Great Controversy*, p. 276.

Now, may I ask you, who is your Father?—God. Who is your mother?—The church; for she is "the woman" whose children we are.

Paul tells us in Galatians 4:26: "Jerusalem which is above is free, which is the mother of us all." But that mother is not only in heaven, she is on earth. Through the sacrifice of Jesus, the family in heaven and the family on earth are one. In Ephesians 3:15, Paul speaks of the Father, "of whom the family in heaven and earth is named." We just witnessed a baptism. Souls were baptized into the name of the Father, the Son, and the Holy Spirit. It is a wonderful thing that you and I are permitted to share that name. But remember that, as members of God's great family, we not only have a Father; we have a mother. God is our Father; the church is our mother. She is "the mother of us all."

In that wonderful vision recorded in Revelation 21, John the Beloved was shown the heavenly Jerusalem. The angel said, "Come hither, I will shew thee the bride, the Lamb's wife." The new Jerusalem, represented as the bride of Christ, is the capital city of His kingdom. But a mere mass of gold and pearl has no attractions for Jesus simply as a pile of material. He has His heart set on filling that city with the citizens of His kingdom. The city is just a setting, a frame if you please; the real thing is the people, His church, a large part of which are still here in the world. There are some in heaven. Enoch is there, and Moses and Elijah, and the great multitude who went with Jesus at the time of His resurrection and ascension. Around the throne of God they stand as evidence that Christ can take human beings that have known the curse of sin and bring them into the kingdom of light. They are perfectly at home; they belong there. They have walked with God here; they walk with Him there. How beautiful is the thought that "the church of God below is one with the church of God above. Believers on the earth and the beings in heaven who have never fallen constitute one church." *Testimonies*, Vol. 3, p. 366.

We have met today for a dedicatory service for this church building. But like the New Jerusalen, this building is meaningless except for the people in it. And, dear friends, it is a wonderful privilege that you and I have, to be the children of the church, as well as the children of God.

If we are like Jesus, what will be our attitude toward the church? We will love the church, as He loves the church. Notice Ephesians 5:25. Christ "loved the church, and gave Himself for it." *The Ministry of Healing*, page 356, says: "Christ honored the marriage relation by making it also a symbol of the union between Him and His redeemed ones. He Himself is the Bridegroom; the bride is the church, of which, as His chosen one, He says, 'Thou art all fair, my love; there is no spot in thee.'" [1]

---

[1] Note: *The Great Controversy*, page 427, presents an apparent difficulty to the view that the church is the bride. Commenting on the parable of the ten virgins, it says: "The bride represents the Holy City, and the virgins that go out to meet the bridegroom are a symbol of the church. In the Revelation the people of God are said to be the guests at the marriage supper. If guests, they cannot be represented also as the bride."

It will be helpful to recall that symbols are sometimes used to represent more than one object. For example, Jesus uses "leaven" to represent "the kingdom of heaven." Matthew 13:33. But He spake also of "the leaven of the Pharisees and Sadducees." Matthew 16:6.

And remember that it is not merely the church triumphant in glory that Christ loves, but the church as it is now. Listen as I read from *Testimonies to Ministers*, page 15: "Dear Brethren of the General Conference: I testify to my brethren and sisters that the church of Christ, enfeebled and defective as it may be, is the only object on earth on which He bestows His supreme regard." That should give us courage for ourselves personally, and it should give us great courage concerning the church, Christ's church in the world. We must never forget that Gethsemane and Calvary were for His church. It was for His church that He poured out His soul in the garden. It was for His church that He gave His life upon the cross.

Now, if there is anyone who thinks that the church can be ignored and God can be dealt with directly leaving the church aside, I say to you, such a one simply does not understand Father. You know, in a properly united home, no child loves one parent and despises the other. If one of the children should say, "Well, I will listen to you, Father, but I don't want to listen to Mother," what would Father say? He would say, "Listen, she is your mother, and she is my wife. And when she says something I want you to love and respect her." That, my friends, is the message of Jesus to every one concerning His church. Christ loves the church, and He wants us to love her.

Somebody may say, "Yes, but what do you mean by the church?" I am dealing with some very practical things, because ahead of us lie great issues. Do you ever get any mimeographed material through the mail? I get a sheet once in a while that presumes to tell me that the church— God's church—simply means faithful souls, no matter whether they belong to some organization or not. And in support of this, *Acts of the Apostles*, page 11 is quoted, which reads like this: "From the beginning, faithful souls have constituted the church."

So we should be able to accept the plain statement that in the parable of the ten virgins the church is not the bride, and also accept the equally plain statements that in other settings the bride represents the church. Note the following from the Ellen G. White comments in *S.D.A. Bible Commentary*, Vol. 7, pp. 985, 986: "God is the husband of His church. The church is the bride, the Lamb's wife." (*Letter* 39, 1902.) The church is the bride, the Lamb's wife. She should keep herself pure, sanctified, holy. Never should she indulge in any foolishness; for she is the bride of a King." (*Letter* 177, 1901.)

Certainly, faithful souls constitute the church. But there is nothing in this statement that teaches that they are to be unorganized or disorganized in order to constitute the true church.

"Like a mighty army moves the church of God." It is not a disorganized mob; it is a well-organized army. And concerning the remnant who receive the Latter Rain and go forward to give the Loud Cry, it is written in *Early Writings*, page 271, that "they moved in exact order like a company of soldiers."

I want to share with you a statement in *Testimonies for the Church*, Vol. 9, pages 257, 258: "O how Satan would rejoice if he could succeed in his efforts to get in among this people and disorganize the work at a time when thorough organization is essential and will be the greatest power to keep out spurious uprisings and to refute claims not endorsed by the Word of God!" Notice that one of the greatest powers to keep out these spurious uprisings will be thorough organization. It is "essential." God wants His people today, as they were when they were led out of Egypt, thoroughly organized. Oh friends, we need both Father and Mother to keep us straight.

May I read a little farther here, in *Testimonies*, Vol. 9, page 258: "Some have advanced the thought that, as we near the close of time, every child of God will act independently of any religious organization. But I have been instructed by the Lord that in this work there is no such thing as every man's being independent." Will we need Father *and Mother* right on through to the end? Yes, indeed.

In Matthew 18, Jesus gave instruction to His disciples concerning church discipline. If someone is not doing right, he is to be labored with, first alone (verse fifteen), then "one or two more" are to be brought in to labor with him. And finally, if he will not hear them, verse seventeen says: "tell it unto the church." To carry out this instruction there must be a definite organized body to whom the matter can be referred. And, if the erring one "neglect to hear the church, let him be unto thee as an heathen man and a publican." God has given His church—His organized church—authority. He says in verse eighteen: "Whatsoever ye shall bind on earth shall be bound in heaven: and whatsoever ye shall loose on earth shall be loosed in heaven." You see, there is something more to this than merely faithful souls all over the world with no organization.

God has a church in this world with authority, yes, a commission given to it: to care for, to nurture, and to discipline the sons and daughters who are the children of God the Father, and also the children of the church, the mother. We honor our mothers in the flesh, the mother who bore us, the mother who nursed us tenderly. And so we should think of the church as the one that has, under God, brought to us the gospel of grace, and has brought us to the point of knowing this wonderful truth, this glorious message. God wants us to acknowledge her authority, to respect and honor her as the bride of Christ and the mother of each one of us.

But suppose I say, "I know what Father wants. I am not going to wait to find out what Mother thinks about it at all. I am just going to do what I believe Father wants me to do." Will that please Father? No! If you would like to read something interesting, as an example of what I am talking about, read in *Testimonies for the Church*, Vol. 5, pages 291-295, the instruction on new light. There the servant of the Lord wrote to a certain man who had been studying the prophecies and had what he thought was new light. He was advised to submit it first "to brethren of experience," and "if they see no light in it, yield to their judgment; for in a multitude of counselors there is safety." If that instruction were followed today, it would save a great deal of confusion.

Let's listen to Mother, friends, for she is dear to the heart of God; and her Husband, who is the Head, has given her authority. And He will not bless those who seek to bypass Mother and ignore her and say, "I am going to deal with Father. I will read the Bible; I will read the Spirit of Prophecy; I will pray all by myself. I will investigate anything I feel impressed to investigate and come to my own conclusions. I do not need advice or warning. I can tell if something is wrong." Ah, what a perilous path! Do you remember how sin entered this world? Do you remember somebody who wanted to investigate? Did she find an answer to her own satisfaction? Yes, she did, but did it lead to joy or to woe? Did it lead to truth or to error? But she did what she wanted—she investigated.

Now, the question may arise, Do you believe the church is infallible? Do you believe that Mother never makes a mistake? Do you believe that the brethren are always right in their counsel? These are fair questions, and they deserve a fair answer, an inspired answer. And that answer is found in *Selected Messages*, Book 1, page 37: "*God alone is infallible.*" It is because we believe this that we are not Roman Catholics. It was Pope Gregory VII who introduced the idea that the church is infallible, "that the church had never erred, nor would it ever err." But the Lord's messenger very aptly adds, "The Scripture proofs did not accompany the assertion." *Great Controversy*, p. 57.

So we do not need to take the position that the church is infallible; in fact, we dare not take that position for that is not what the Bible teaches. But when we say that the church is not infallible we are admitting that the church—the majority of the church—could be mistaken on some point. We have to recognize that human beings are human beings, and when they give counsel, it could be a mistake. It has happened. But all this does not lessen the force of what we are studying together. God, when He selected Mother, knew that she was not infallible. God did not choose His church because its members individually or collectively were infallible. Jesus knew all about you and me, and He knew all about the church. But "from heaven He came and sought her to be His holy bride." And if we will think of the church as Jesus thinks of her, we will love her as Jesus loves her and we will listen to her with deference and respect. This will please Him.

Now Father has cautioned Mother against this Roman Catholic idea of thinking that the church is infallible. Paul warned in 2 Thessalonians 2:1-8, against the apostasy which was already working in the apostolic church. By the searchlight of prophecy, Paul discerned that this apostasy would eventually result in the mystery of iniquity when man would sit in the temple of God, in the place of God, "showing himself that he is God." That is what the papal apostasy is—it is the church putting itself in the place of God. It is Mother trying to take Father's place. That does not work well in any family. There is a divine harmony in heaven's plan of organization, in individual families and in the church. Mother has plenty to do in the place to which she has been assigned in heaven. When she seeks to get out of that place and to fill Father's place it is just too much. When the Roman church thought itself able to tamper with the law of God it stepped clear out of the divinely-appointed place of Mother, and attempted to take Father's place, and God disowned her.

Today, in the true church we are warned against any such thing creeping in. Remember there was a time when the early church was pure; but this spirit of human authority brought the papacy. And today we are warned against it. Satan "works to restrict religious liberty and to bring into the religious world a species of slavery. Organizations, institutions, unless kept by the power of God, will work under Satan's dictation to bring men under the control of men and fraud and guile will bear the semblance of zeal for truth and for the advancement of the kingdom of God....

"If men resist the warnings the Lord sends them, they become even leaders in evil practices; such men assume to exercise the prerogatives of God they presume to do that which God Himself will not do in seeking to control the minds of men. Thus they follow in the track of Romanism." *Testimonies*, Vol. 7, pp. 180, 181.

Every one of us as children needs to remember to respect God's authority and to respect the authority He has committed to His church. Every one of us as a part of that church which exercises authority over its members needs to be careful lest we get over on the Father's side of the authority and seek to assume prerogatives that belong to God alone. The warning is clear on both sides.

Let us go back to the book of Exodus, to a striking example of the proper attitude toward God's truth, God's church, God's movement. The man that is the hero of this story is Moses; and I want you to remember that there are some people down here today that are going to sing the song of Moses. In Exodus 32, we see Moses on Mount Sinai. He has been up there for many days getting the directions for the sanctuary. Down in the plain, Aaron is in charge. The people have gotten restless. They are asking for a golden calf. And finally they get what they want, because Aaron seems to believe that the voice of the people is the voice of God.

Let me ask you, was it the majority of the people that wanted it? Oh yes, a great majority. Was Aaron a popular leader? Yes, he was! Things were going well, except for a few people that thought God was being dishonored. We are told that some of them lost their lives in standing against the apostasy. (See *Patriarchs and Prophets*, p. 316).

But on the mountain Moses knew nothing of all this. He was shut in with God. Finally the Lord told him, "Moses, the people down there have made a golden calf and they are dancing around it and having a riotous feast; they have gone back into Egyptian idolatry. And Moses, I am so grieved with them, I am so disappointed, and I am so displeased, that I have reached the point where I am going to destroy all of them. And Moses, I am going to let you be the nucleus of a great reform movement which will take the place of the apostate people."

And what did Moses say? Did he say, "Well, Lord, I feel sorry that it has to be that way, but if You see that that's all that can be done, all right." Is that what he said? Did he say, "Lord, they have already made me a lot of trouble, and if you see that the time has come to disown them and put them away, then Lord, I will do my best to have some people that never disappoint you." Is that what Moses said? No. Moses had caught something of this love that Christ has for the church.

Down on his knees, on his face, he pled for Israel. He reminded the Lord of His promises; he reminded Him of what the heathen would say if that movement, that church, should fail; and finally in his desperate love for those people, he said, "Lord, if You cannot forgive them, blot me, I pray Thee, out of Thy book." Exodus 32:32. Read the whole chapter, friends, and the next, and the next ... and get that picture of Moses— offered the opportunity to become the nucleus of a new movement, but instead, interceding for Israel. Did God hear his prayer? Was Israel saved? Did the movement go through? Yes, yes, yes.

So today, whatever weakness or worldliness we may find in the church, let us never think that those who are ready to leave the movement or denounce the movement have the spirit of Jesus. Thank God, there will be those today like Moses who on their knees will intercede for Israel.

They will draw God and His church together in the arms of faith and love. And they will sing *the song of Moses*.

Look at Jesus in Gethsemane. What was the great burden of His heart? It was that His church and His Father might be brought together, held together, in a union that could never be dissolved. But Satan pressed upon Him the terrible temptation that if He held on to His church He would lose God forever. On the other hand, He could let go of His people and go back to heaven and be with His Father. And what did Jesus do? Ah, friends, He wouldn't let go of either one. With the hand of faith He clung to His Father, even though He couldn't see Him; with the other hand, love, He clung to His people, His church, and He wouldn't let go! And as He engaged in that mighty struggle, in the garden and on the cross, it seemed that He would be torn apart. He *was* torn apart. His heart was broken. But He would not let go of either one; those who understand something of that broken heart in Gethsemane and Calvary will share with Jesus the consuming burden for the church and God to stay together. They will never consent to any separation. With one hand on God and one hand on the church, they will pull together. The result will be that while in the coming crisis there will be a "mighty sifting" (*Testimonies for the Church*, Vol. 5, p. 80), yet the church will go through triumphantly.

Oh, friends! Those who sing the song of Moses will also sing *the song of the Lamb*—the brokenhearted Lamb, the Lamb in whose blood the church is purged. Heart to heart with Jesus here, they will be closest to Him through eternity.

And may I say to you now, this is a sermon not merely for tomorrow; this is a sermon for today. We are even now, dear ones, in the shaking time referred to in *Early Writings*, pages 269 and 270. We are entering the day described in *Testimonies for the Church*, Vol. 5, p. 80, when there is great perplexity and confusion; every wind of doctrine is blowing, there are gods many and lords many.

And listen! I fear for those children of the church who are too ready to ignore what Father has said, clinging to Mother and saying, "We'll just do what Mother does and listen to what Mother says. And what God has said through the Bible and the Spirit of Prophecy, we'll let Mother answer for." I'm afraid of that, friends. And may I tell you I am equally afraid for those children who say, "We'll listen to Father and we won't pay very much attention to Mother." I fear for those who seem to be so ready to find some excuse, if not to *defy* the voice of the church, at least to ignore it.

God help us, friends; it's a narrow road that we must walk. We are in the time when these very problems that we are studying must drive the true people of God to their knees, seeking for that light and blessing which will enable them to find their way amid the confusion of voices that say, "lo here" and, "lo there."

Personally, friends, I need Father; I need Mother. I must have them both to help me on the heavenward way. And I love them both. In the words of that sweet old hymn:

> "I love Thy kingdom Lord,
> The house of Thine abode:
> The church our blessed Redeemer saved
> With His own precious blood.
>
> "I love Thy church O God;
> Her walls before Thee stand
> Dear as the apple of Thine eye
> And graven on Thy hand.
>
> "For her my tears shall fall,
> For her my prayers ascend;
> To her my cares and toils be given
> Till toils and cares shall end.
>
> "Beyond my highest joy
> I prize her heavenly ways;
> Her sweet communion, solemn vows,
> Her hymns of love and praise.
>
> "Sure as Thy truth shall last,
> To Zion shall be given
> The brightest glories earth can yield
> And brighter bliss of heaven."

Now, some very practical things. Suppose Mother seems to make a mistake. What should we do? Think of it in the home. What would you do with your own mother if you were old enough to understand right from wrong, and you saw her making some mistake? Wouldn't you plead with her? I hope you wouldn't "tell her off" or stand up in impudence and say, "*I* know what Father said, and Mother, you are not doing it." I don't think Father would appreciate that; and I know Mother wouldn't appreciate it. Thank God, there is a better way. Plead with your mother. And I ask you, who will have influence with Mother? The loving, respectful child, not the impudent one who is watching for a chance to prove that Mother is off the track.

Now, friends, in this last generation, because we have special needs, because we are to reach special heights, Christ has sent His church—the mother and her children—some special messages. Have you read them? Here are these books, *Testimonies for the Church*. You will find many pages that deal with the church as a group. Many pages deal with the individual members. Here are the love letters of the great Father above, written to Mother and the children. Ah, friends, would it not be a good thing for Mother and the children to be reading them every day? To get them into action, doing what they say? As we do that, we will make Father happy. Oh, how glad He is when He sees His church busily reading the messages He has sent from heaven, and carrying them out in the life.

I pray that God may greatly bless every one of you as you endeavor to fill your home and your heart with these precious messages. Thus we shall be helping to answer the prayer of Jesus that His church may be prepared for His coming. How wonderful it will be to share in the glad reunion when Mother and all the children are at home with Father forever.

ADDITIONAL QUOTATIONS

"Very close and sacred is the relation between Christ and His church,—He the bridegroom, and the church the bride; He the head, and the church the body. Connection with Christ, then, involves connection with His church." *Education*, p. 268.

"God has made His church on the earth a channel of light, and through it He communicates His purposes and His will. He does not give to one of His servants an experience independent of and contrary to the experience of the church itself. Neither does He give one man a knowledge of His will for the entire church, while the church—Christ's body—is left in darkness. In His providence, He places His servants in close connection with His church, in order that they may have less confidence in themselves, and greater confidence in others whom He is leading out to advance His work.

"There have ever been in the church those who are constantly inclined toward individual independence. They seem unable to realize that independence of spirit is liable to lead the human agent to have too much confidence in himself, and to trust in his own judgment rather than to respect the counsel and highly esteem the judgment of his brethren, especially those in the offices that God has appointed for the leadership of His people. God has invested His church with special authority and power, which no one can be justified in disregarding and despising; for he who does this despises the voice of God.

"Those who are inclined to regard their individual judgment as supreme, are in grave peril. It is Satan's studied effort to separate such ones from those who are channels of light, through whom God has wrought to build up and extend His work in the earth. To neglect or despise those whom God has appointed to bear the responsibilities of leadership in connection with the advancement of the truth, is to reject the means that He has ordained for the help, encouragement, and strength of His people. For any worker in the Lord's cause to pass these by, and to think that his light must come through no other channel than directly from God, is to place himself in a position where he is liable to be deceived by the enemy, and overthrown." *Acts of the Apostles*, pp. 163, 164.

"In the commission to His disciples, Christ not only outlined their work, but gave them their message. 'Teach the people,' He said, 'to observe all things whatsoever I have commanded you.' The disciples were to teach what Christ had taught. That which He had spoken, not only in person, but through all the prophets and teachers of the Old Testament, is here included. Human teaching is shut out. There is no place for tradition, for man's theories and conclusions, or for church legislation. No laws ordained by ecclesiastical authority are included in the commission. None of these are Christ's servants to teach." *Desire of Ages*, p. 826.

"The church organization is to be respected, but it is not to be made in any way a galling yoke. Men are not to assume the prerogative of God, and think to rule and coerce and oppress the souls of God's purchased possession....

"O that men would revere the great Head of the church, and would manufacture less human methods, bringing down spirituality to the very dust with human inventions! God has been left out, and the church is not prepared to advance to the conflict under the banner of Jesus Christ. It is not doing the work for suffering souls, which Christ owns as if done to Himself. But the church, defective as it is, and enfeebled with so much chaff, is the only object on earth upon which He bestows His highest regard. In His estimation, the church in heaven and the church on earth are identical." Ellen G. White, *Manuscript* 43, 1895 (quoted by C.C. Crisler in *Organization*, pp. 129, 130).

"God has a church on earth who are lifting up the downtrodden law, and presenting to the world the Lamb of God that taketh away the sins of the world. The church is the depository of the wealth of the riches of the grace of Christ, and through the church eventually will be made manifest the final and full display of the love of God to the world that is to be lightened with its glory. The prayer of Christ that His church may be one as He was one with His Father will finally be answered." *Testimonies to Ministers*, p. 50.

MINISTRY OF HERESIES

"And we know that all things work together for good to them that love God, to them who are the called according to His purpose." Rom. 8:28.

What do all things do? They work together. As we view them here in this world they seem to be working at cross purposes, but all things are working together. And they are working together for good, not for everybody, but for those who love the Lord. Man has been given the power of choice. It rests with each one whether everything that is working together is working together for his personal good or not. But we must never lose sight of the eventual triumph of God's purpose, the eventual carrying out of His plan. And we must never for a minute forget that those forces which seem to bring defeat are nevertheless being used by God. "All things work together for good."

Notice how Paul speaks of this in 2 Cor. 13:8: "For we can do nothing against the truth, but for the truth." Isn't that wonderful! Even the devil can't do anything really against the truth. He is trying all the time, and here in this world he seems to be having his way. But let us look behind the scenes. God is working out His will. "We can do nothing against the truth."

In the great crisis that is ahead of the church—which it is even now entering—we shall need the wisdom as well as the courage that comes from reminding ourselves of these promises.

"Surely the wrath of man shall praise thee: the remainder of wrath shalt thou restrain." (Ps. 76:10). God uses even the wrath of man to praise Him. Now man shouldn't get any credit for that. But God should get a great deal of credit for using even the plans of His enemies and the wrath of the dragon to work out His will. And any wrath that doesn't praise Him, He restrains.

Now this is no credit to Satan or his devils, and it is no credit to human beings that are used by him. They must all suffer in the final judgment for their rebellion against God and for the specious theories which they have advocated. They are just as guilty as though they had succeeded in subverting the truth of God and unseating God from His throne. But they cannot succeed.

Concerning the security of His children Jesus says, "No man is able to pluck them out of My Father's hand." (John 10:29). We can be glad for that.

I've been led to study this subject as I have contemplated this inspiring statement from the messenger of the Lord in an article in the *Signs of the Times*, January 6, 1898. "It is thought by some to be a misfortune when erroneous theories are advanced, but the Lord has said, 'All things work together for good to them that love God.' The contention among the Corinthians made it necessary for Paul to write his wonderful epistles to them. If the Gentiles had not backslidden from the faith, Paul would not have written, "I marvel that ye are so soon removed from Him that called you into the grace of Christ unto another gospel, which is not another.' It was a misapplication of the Scriptures, to prove falsehood and error true. If the Thessalonians had not misinterpreted the instruction they received, they would not have entertained the belief that the Lord was immediately to be revealed in the clouds of heaven, thus making it necessary for Paul to present the truth as it is in Jesus, leaving on record truth important for all time. And so opposition against light and truth called from Christ a clearer definition of the truth. Every time that error is advanced, it will work for good to those who sincerely love God; for when the truth is shadowed by error, those whom the Lord has made His sentinels will make the truth sharper and clearer. They will search the Scriptures for evidence of their faith. The advancement of error is the call for God's servants to arouse, and place the truth in bold relief."

So, this morning, I want to study with you why God allows erroneous theories to come to His church either from without or from within. For the Scriptures state clearly that both happen. Paul said, "Grievous wolves" shall "enter in among you, not sparing the flock. Also of your own selves shall men arise, speaking perverse things, to draw away disciples after them." Acts 20:29, 30.

Why does God allow His church to be rent and torn with schism, factions, contentions, discussion over this and that point? Why is the unity of the church threatened at times by these things? You can see already from the texts we have read that God must have a purpose or He wouldn't allow it.

Let us look at three great purposes accomplished through the ministry of heresies, three objectives that God has in mind in allowing erroneous theories of various kinds to find their way to you and me. God could stop them. Why does He let them come? As we study the ministry of heresies we shall find at least three answers.

The first is, *to sift out the false-hearted.*

"Little children, it is the last time: and as ye have heard that anti-Christ shall come, even now are there many anti-christs; whereby we know that it is the last time. They went out from us, but they were not of us; for if they had been of us, they would no doubt have continued with us: but they went out, and that they might be made manifest that they were not all of us." (1 John 2:18, 19). The false-hearted went out. Why? That it might be made manifest—that is, *clearly revealed*—that they were not of us.

Notice this wonderful statement on heresies by the servant of the Lord in *Testimonies*, Vol. 5, p. 707: "God will arouse His people, if other means fail, heresies will come in among them, which will sift them, separating the chaff from the wheat."

What do heresies do? They sift the church! What happens to the chaff? It is separated from the wheat! Never forget, that as the winds blow, whether they be the winds of heresy or the winds of persecution, it's the chaff that goes out; it's the wheat that remains.

When I was visiting in Florida, a friend took me over to the packing shed where they were sorting oranges according to size. The oranges were on a chute and as they passed over a certain place there were little holes and the tiniest oranges dropped through these holes. Presently, as the oranges went along there were holes a little larger and the little larger oranges went through there and so on. Dear friends, just because you are not fooled with one heresy be careful how you pat yourself on the back. In my imagination I have looked at those oranges coming along and I've heard a medium sized orange say, "Well, we are not going to fall through. We've already been through that test and this one and we didn't fall through. We are going right on through to the end." But they haven't been clear through the sieve yet.

Some of the heresies that the devil brings in are so crude and bungling that it is amazing to me that they fool anybody. But the devil is not through the work of bringing heresies among God's people and God is not through allowing him to do it. Some far more subtle, more seductive, more difficult to discern and detect than we have ever yet seen are doubtless on the planning boards of the devil's corporation. He is studying your mind and character and if there is anything false-hearted there he will design something that will sift you out. Our only safeguard is to be sure that we are anchored in Jesus and His truth and that we love God and His church more than we love ourselves and our own opinions.

Now, there is another purpose of the ministry of heresies. I trust that God will use this to bless some heart who might feel secure, who might be secure as far as theology is concerned. We get it from the story of Jehu, one of the kings of Israel.

Let us get a picture of Jehu from the sacred record: "And the driving is like the driving of Jehu, the son of Nimshi; for he driveth furiously." (2 Kings 9:20). *Jehu was a driver*. He has descendents today. He was furious against the apostasy and heresy of Ahab and rightly so, but there was something that he lacked. He lacked love.

Jehu was full of zeal. Watch him in action. "When he was departed thence, he lighted on Jehonadab the son of Rechab coming to meet him: and he saluted him, and said to him, Is thine heart right, as my heart is with thy heart? And Jehonadab answered, It is. If it be, give me thine hand. And he gave him his hand; and took him up to him into the chariot. And he said, *Come with me, and see my zeal for the Lord*. So they made him ride in his chariot. And when He came to Samaria, he slew all that remained unto Ahab in Samaria, till he had destroyed him, according to the saying of the Lord, which he spake to Elijah." 2 Kings 10:15-17.

Jehu was doing God's work but not in God's way. Yet God was using him. Baal worship needed to be rooted out and Jehu was the man for the job; but I am afraid we won't see Jehu in heaven.

Now I am calling attention to this because I read something in the book *Testimonies to Ministers*, page 333: "All who are longing for some engagement that will represent Jehu riding furiously will have opportunity enough to distinguish themselves."

So Jehu's chariot is still riding. And like Jehu of old, there are some today who will stop the chariot just long enough to say, "Is your heart right as my heart is? If it is get in and ride with me, we're going to go places and destroy Baal worship in Israel. Let me show you my zeal for the Lord."

Notice this inspired comment, an Ellen G. White statement in *S.D.A. Bible Commentary*, volume 2, page 1038: "Men are slow to learn the lesson that the spirit manifested by Jehu will never bind hearts together. It is not safe for us to bind our interests with a Jehu religion, for this will result in bringing sadness of heart on God's true worshipers. God has not given to any of His servants the work of punishing those who would not heed His warnings and reproofs. When the Holy Spirit is abiding in the heart it will lead the human agent to see his own defects of character, to pity the weakness of others, to forgive as he wishes to be forgiven."

Part of the ministry of heresies is to give opportunity for Jehu to manifest himself. But because we see some in the church rising up militantly to defend the faith, to get out their swords and ride in the chariot zealously, is no evidence that they will be with God's people at the finish.

Note the warning in *Testimonies*, Vol. 6, p. 400: "As trials thicken around us, both separation and unity will be seen in our ranks. Some who are now ready to take up weapons of warfare will in times of real peril make it manifest that they have not built upon the solid rock; they will yield to temptation. Those who have had great light and precious privileges, but have not improved them, will under one pretext or another, go out from us."

There is more than one way to go out. We can get out the way Ahab got out and we can get out the way Jehu got out. God keep us from either path of peril. But, remember, God was using them all.

Now there is a third ministry of heresies. Oh, I wish every one of us here might be among those for whom it accomplishes this third purpose—*to lead us to study the word of God*. Concerning those in Berea, the Scripture says, "These were more noble than those in Thessalonica, in that they received the word with all readiness of mind, and searched the Scriptures daily whether those things were so." (Acts 17:11).

In *Testimonies*, Vol. 5, p. 707, we are told: "There are many in the church who take it for granted that they understand what they believe; but until controversy arises, they do not know their own weakness."

"The fact that there is no controversy or agitation among God's professed people should not be regarded as conclusive evidence that they are holding fast to sound doctrine. There is reason to fear that they may not be clearly discriminating between truth and error. When no new questions are started by investigation of the Scriptures, when no difference of opinion arises which will set men to searching the Bible for themselves to make sure that they have the truth, there will be many now, as in ancient times, who will hold to tradition and worship they know not what."

So one of the reasons that God allows erroneous theories of various kinds to come in is to lead us to go to the word of God and to study for ourselves what God has said. If heresies accomplish that, has not some good been accomplished?

We need more than a superficial knowledge of the Bible. Satan is adept at quoting Scripture. In the wilderness his first temptation was met by Jesus from the Word. Satan said, "I can do that too." So in the second temptation he quoted from the Scriptures. Merely because a man quotes Scripture does not mean he is teaching truth. Just because he gets out leaflets and mimeographed material liberally sprinkled with quotations from the Spirit of Prophecy doesn't prove that he is an angel of light.

Oh my friends, this may be the most important thing in my sermon for some of you—*what we need to study most of all is the original sources, the Bible and the Spirit of Prophecy.*

Notice this statement in *Testimonies*, Vol. 8, p. 298: "Perilous times are before us.... The enemy is on our track. We must be wide awake, on our guard against him....We must follow the directions given through the Spirit of Prophecy. We must love and obey the truth for this time. This will save us from accepting strong delusions. God has spoken to us through His word. He has spoken to us through the testimonies to the church and through the books that have helped to make plain our present duty and the position that we should now occupy. ...

"I beseech those who are laboring for God not to accept the spurious for the genuine. Let not human reason be placed where divine, sanctifying truth should be.... Let not erroneous theories receive countenance from the people who ought to be standing firm on the platform of eternal truth."

Down through the history of this movement, there have been good men, educated men, experienced men, that have lost their way and fallen on the dark mountains of unbelief because the enemy succeeded in leading them away from the truth even while they thought they were pursuing truth with all their heart.

We need God. We need the help of our brethren. We need the Holy Spirit. We need to dig deep into the written word and the inspired commentary of the Spirit of Prophecy. In *Testimonies*, Vol. 5, p. 273, is this statement: "Our people need to understand the oracles of God; they need to have a systematic knowledge of the principles of revealed truth, which will fit them for what is coming upon the earth and prevent them from being carried about by every wind of doctrine."

God allows these false teachings and heresies in order to get you and me to study into the original sources and to get *a systematic knowledge* of the principles of truth. We need to see how the different principles fit together, to get them woven into our mind into a tapestry of truth; to get them built into a solid temple of truth; to have on every piece of the heavenly armor for we shall need it in the battle in which we are now engaged.

Several years ago, the United States government conducted schools in various parts of the country to teach bank cashiers and others how to detect counterfeit money. The instruction lasted for fourteen weeks. How many pieces of counterfeit money did they examine? Not one! The government instructor knew that what they needed was *a thorough knowledge of the genuine*. Then they could detect the counterfeit.

If you and I are going to be saved from the many erroneous theories that are floating around, we need to study the original sources, filling our minds with the Bible and the Spirit of Prophecy. We will never find our safety in going into these false theories and studying them over and over. The better we know the genuine, the more surely will we detect the counterfeit when we meet it.

Oh that God may solemnize our hearts, that we may not be so wise in our own conceits, so sure of our own opinions or the opinions of others, that we fail to get down on our knees as little children and say, "Dear Lord, there is much I don't know. I want to know You and Your way. Oh keep me from the delusions of the enemy." We shall need to pray that prayer again and again. We shall need to intercede with God, for we are entering into the time foretold in *Testimonies*, Vol. 5, p. 80: "Every wind of doctrine will be blowing."

"If we would not have the Scriptures clouded to our understanding, so that the plainest truths shall not be comprehended, we must have the simplicity and faith of a little child, ready to learn, and beseeching the aid of the Holy Spirit." *Testimonies*, Vol. 5, p. 703.

ANOTHER ARK TO BUILD

Jesus says that "as the days of Noah were, so shall also the coming of the Son of man be." Has He given a message to the world today like the message of Noah? Is the world going to be destroyed? Yes, it is. And has God sent some people into the world to preach as Noah preached? Has God sent out any of you to do what Noah was sent to do? Some of you know that you have been called. I hope that others will hear the call and enter into it, too, because we were born for nothing else, my dear friends, but to give a message similar to Noah's message, in no uncertain tones. But Noah's preaching is not my subject here. My subject is Noah's ark-building. "By faith Noah, being warned of God of things not seen as yet, moved with fear, prepared an ark to the saving of his house."

Noah not only preached he worked. He worked with his hands. He had to bring those mighty trees down to the ground, make them up into timbers, and put them together in that great boat. It was quite a piece of engineering!

And God's purpose in telling Noah to build it was to provide a way of escape—a refuge from the storm that was coming. Did anybody escape as the result of that ark being built? Yes. In fact, the only people who survived the flood, survived as a result of Noah's ark-building!

Oh friends, the present time is as the days of Noah. You know the world is not preparing for what is coming. As in the days of Noah they ate and drank, they planted and they builded, they married and were given in marriage; and likewise today this country is in the greatest spending spree of history. The feeling is, "People never had it so good." That's the way it was in the days of Noah.

The labor unions are coming into the picture larger and larger. Not long ago the two great branches of the labor movement combined to form one great union. When that happened we read over the prophecies and we said, "This will mean something in the history of America and the world. Here is an enormous new factor—a political power—thirteen million working men and women welded into one great movement. Things can happen now that couldn't have happened here before."

We didn't have to be profound thinkers to predict that something might happen. You and I have been given special light from heaven that it is largely through the labor unions that the persecutions, Sunday laws, and boycotts of Revelation 13 are going to be fulfilled. (You will find that in *Selected Messages*, Book 2.) We saw this great new power—the AFL-CIO—come onto the scene and we began to look for results. Some of those results are here already—politically, legislatively, industrially, and financially.

Over a hundred years ago, the Lord's messenger pointed forward to the time when in all our great cities there would be a binding up in bundles by the confederacies and unions formed. The lives of those who refused to unite with these unions would be imperiled. And then she said that the same binding up in unions that exists today existed in Noah's day.

So Noah faced these same problems. But following God's directions led him safely through every problem.

Now, let me ask you, Is there need for an ark today? At the coming of Jesus we know that we will be taken away from every danger and go up to heaven. We are going to leave the world. We won't need any ark to get through that experience.

There's a great time of trouble just preceding that, when the plagues will be falling, when many of God's people will be in the caves and the rocks of the mountains. How are we going to get along then? Oh, the angels are going to feed us! You can read that in *Early Writings*, page 56. How we're going to get out of the world I think we all understand. How we're going to live through that awful time of trouble is quite clear. But there is a time before that called the "little time of trouble" that comes before probation closes; a time of peril and persecution that follows swiftly after the national Sunday law is passed. How will we get through that?

Let's look at that time in the 13th chapter of Revelation. Verse 16 speaks of the two-horned beast, the symbol of the United States: "And he causeth all, both small and great, rich and poor, free and bond, to receive a mark in their right hand, or in their foreheads."

Are you going to receive that mark? You aren't? Well, then, what will happen to you? The 17th verse: "And that no man might buy or sell, save he that had the mark, or the name of the beast, or the number of his name."

Will you take the mark? No. For God says in the 14th chapter of Revelation that you must not do it. You will drink the wine of the wrath of God if you do. And in the 15th chapter and the second verse, John sees in heaven the company of saints who have gotten the victory over the beast, and his image, and his mark, and the number of his name. They haven't taken the mark, have they?

Now, my question is this, friends. If there is coming a time before the close of probation when you cannot buy anything to eat, of what help is it going to be to you to have a promise that angels will feed you at some later time in a cave, if you starve to death before that? Is that a practical question?

There was a rainbow on the other side of the flood, but the great thing, when the rain began to fall, was how to get through that flood! There is a storm coming just ahead and many people have little idea how they are going to get through it. And I am afraid the attitude of some is, "Well, the Lord will take us through somehow." In other words, they expect to get through the little time of trouble exactly the way they will get through that great time of trouble when the plagues are falling.

Now suppose Noah had gone about preaching and saying, "There's a flood coming! Get ready for it!" And suppose the people had said, "If a flood is coming, what are we going to do?" Just suppose that Noah had answered, "Oh, the Lord will take care of us somehow."

And picture him saying to his sons, "We just haven't any time to build a boat, because it's so important to get out and preach and tell the people that the flood is coming." That would not have been logical, would it? It would not have been obedience, either.

Who told Noah the flood was coming? God did. And He told him to preach. But He also said, "Build an ark." Noah was to practice what he preached. He was to preach what he was practicing. It was all tied up together.

Hear this wonderful statement from *Story of Redemption*, page 63: "He was not only to preach, but his example in building the ark was to convince all that he believed what he preached. ... *Every blow struck upon the ark was preaching to the people.* Noah directed, he preached, he worked, while the people looked on in amazement and regarded him as a fanatic." You see, Noah preached with his hammer as well as with his vocal chords!

Now, I wonder if God has given you and me any hammering to do while we are preaching and warning people about that storm of persecution that is coming. Is there some practical work involved in preparing for that awful boycott when thousands will be confronted on the one side with the seal of God and on the other with the mark of the beast? I believe there is an answer to that. I find part of it in *Selected Messages*, Book 2. On page 141, the servant of the Lord says: "The time is fast coming when the controlling power of the labor unions will be very oppressive. Again and again the Lord has instructed that our people are to take their families away from the cities, into the country, where they can raise their own provisions; for in the future the problem of buying and selling will be a very serious one."

I am glad that is put in such simple language that anybody can understand it. Let's start with the last thing it says: "The problem of buying and selling will be a very serious one." We won't be able to buy or sell, the Bible tells us, unless we take the mark of the beast. And page 142 of this book tells us that the labor unions are going to have much to do with it.

Now, in view of that, what does Inspiration say we ought to do? Get out of the cities. Get into the country. Move out. Then what are we to do in the country? We are to raise our own provisions—our own food. Page 310 of *Medical Ministry* says, "To parents who are living in the cities, the Lord is sending the warning cry, Gather your children into your own houses; ... Get out of the cities as fast as possible. Parents can secure small homes in the country, with land for cultivation where they can have orchards and where they can raise vegetables and small fruits. ... God will help His people to find such homes outside the cities. As far as possible, our institutions should be located away from the cities. ... It is not God's will that His people shall settle in the cities. ... The Lord desires His people to move into the country where they can settle on the land and raise their own fruit and vegetables."

Friends, you see this is how the Lord plans for us to get through this preliminary time of trouble. This is the way He plans for us to have something to eat when we can't buy or sell, giving us a place of refuge in that time when our lives would be in danger in the cities.

So God has three ways of caring for us in three different stages of the final events: At the very end He will take us clear away from the world. Before that, in the great time of trouble, angels will feed us. But in this first time of trouble we are to get our food by growing it ourselves on the land.

Here is a little tract entitled, *The Nashville Agricultural and Normal Institute* (that's the Madison School) published by the Pacific Press in 1908. It was gotten out by Elder W. C. White. On page 11 Professor Magan says: "At first we felt that the school farm was too large. We had planned, in our own minds, an ideal school farm which should be small, but kept so clean and orderly that it would be a model. ... When we told Sister White our objections to the size of the farm, she said that the time would come when many that are now living in the cities would be forced to leave in order to live the truth, and that we should make the farm a place of refuge where some of these could stop for a while and be taught how to make a living from the soil. Then they would have courage to go out into the country where they could find land, make a home, and educate their children in harmony with God's law."

That is the "ark," friends. There it is! When the storm breaks, when the national Sunday law is passed; when the labor unions are carrying on their oppressive, coercive work; when the Loud Cry is being given and the saints are being hurried out of Sodom, they will need "a place of refuge." Oh, let's build an ark for these dear people!

Let me ask you, Do you think this preliminary time of trouble is going to last for more than a few days or weeks? Why, you can't even grow carrots and harvest them in just a few days. It takes several months to grow sweet potatoes, doesn't it? It takes longer than that to grow strawberries and other small fruits that we have been reading about.

Noah's message was practical. God help us to see that, and if we have a Bible in one hand, to have a hammer or a hoe in the other hand. And we had better know how to use them all—the Bible, the hoe, and the hammer! That is the only way we can "make the farm a place of refuge where some of these could stop for awhile and be taught how to make a living from the soil."

"A place of refuge." The Lord wouldn't tell us to make a place of refuge if there were no refugees going to come to it. Friends, it seems to me that we need to do all our work with that view in our minds—the coming of the refugees. They are coming. God knows they are coming, whether we get ready for them or not.

It must have been a wonderful feeling for Shem, Ham, and Japheth as they saw those two elephants come walking up the gangplank. Can't you hear Noah saying, "Boys, here come the elephants"? And they could answer, "Right this way. We'll put them right down here!"

And what was there, waiting for them? Why, there was hay. Of course there was. The ark was stored with provisions. They were expecting them, don't you see?

When the refugees come, will you have a place for them? And will there be something in the garden and in the granary? Or will you say, "Oh, I'm so sorry! I just don't have any place to take anybody. I don't have food ready to feed anybody." Oh, we had better be ready because the One who knows says they are coming.

Now notice, it takes more than merely living in the country to meet this problem. These refugees are coming out of the cities, and they are coming out to these farms in the country because of a serious problem. They can't buy anything. They can't sell. Now let us think about our vehicle that goes into town to buy groceries for us. What are we going to do when that well runs dry? That is the question we are going to face. There will be more people to be fed; but no place for our buyer to go to get us what we need.

Now, the answer isn't for us to say, "I'll never order another penny's worth!" The time of trouble isn't here yet, but wouldn't it be practical to think about it when we start to make up a shopping list? To ask, "What am I going to do about this item when I can't buy it any more?" That is part of building the ark. It isn't only putting up some buildings to house the refugees; it's planting gardens, berry patches, and fields of corn and sweet potatoes—not only that we may have some food, but that we may have the "know how" to teach the folks who come. Will some of them need to be taught?

Wouldn't it be a wonderful thing if some morning the manager would say to you, "Brother, last night some refugees came in from Chicago, and we would like you to take Brother Smith out—he's been working in a factory and he doesn't know anything about the land—and we would like you to show him how to get a living from the soil."

What would you say? "Oh, you will have to send him to the farm manager!" Or, "Better turn him over to one of the farm boys. I don't know anything about growing food. I just eat the stuff, that's all."

Oh, let's build the ark, what do you say? Let's keep the saw mill running. Let's put up simple buildings,—modest, comfortable, with room enough to take in an extra family or two. And every time we build, let's remember—the refugees are coming. If we plant a garden or an orchard, remember the refugees, because the Lord has told us they are coming.

My friends, if you and I ever act upon this instruction, we will act upon it by faith, in advance of the storm. There were millions, remember, who were convinced of Noah's wisdom when it was too late. I thank God that the Holy Spirit is moving upon us to build this ark *before* it is too late.

But, what kind of an ark is this that we are building? Where do we get the blueprint and the orders? What is it going to look like when we get it done? You can look in this book, *Medical Ministry*, and see the whole picture on pages 308 and 309. The "ark" is a complete little program that God gave our people to establish outside every city; a farm, a school on that farm, a little sanitarium connected with it, an evangelistic center. It is all there.

And God is calling, not only for little institutions. He wants every home to be a place of refuge. Read *Ministry of Healing*, pages 192 to 194.

You farmers, there is work for you. You who are builders and you who are mechanics and you women who know how to cook, how to sew, how to nurse; there is work for you. Read it there. Let God fill your souls with the determination to make your homes places of refuge in the coming crisis.

Do you remember how the allied armies got off the beach at Dunkirk, when the axis forces seemed to have every way of escape cut off? When the big ships were under fire and it looked like doom for those thousands of men? Well, God had an ark of safety for those men— the little yachts and fishing craft of England! Some could take ten men; some could pack in fifty or more. Every size and speed and capacity was there. Little boats plying back and forth in the fog—they moved an army, friends! They saved the lives of an army, those little boats. Hundreds of them. That is the picture.

But those boats had to be there when the crisis came. They had to be seaworthy and loaded with fuel for the voyage. They had to be ready for the rescue. That preparation cost something, didn't it?

Did it cost Noah anything to build the ark? I was reading something on that right here in *Patriarchs and Prophets,* on page 95: "He gave the world an example of believing just what God says. All that he possessed he invested in the ark."

How much? "All that he possessed." Did there come a time when he had to call the family together and say, "Listen, folks, we are going to have to draw out that last money we have in the bank to get another keg of nails"? All that he had he invested.

Furniture, carpets, houses and land—all that he had he invested in the ark. The people of that time were sure that he was a crazy man, that "religion had gone to his head." But when the rain began to fall, and the waters began to rise, and men were throwing their money everywhere in wild desperation as the flood rose around them, Noah didn't have the sorrow of seeing any greenbacks that belonged to him floating on those billows. Not one. There wasn't anything that belonged to Noah that perished in the flood. Nothing.

You say, "How do you know that?" I just read it here: "All that he possessed he invested in the ark." Where was it? It was in the ark. Well, that is where Noah was. Noah was right there with everything he possessed, right there in the ark!

Oh, let us concentrate on getting the ark built, even if it takes everything we have. And let's put all the parts together according to the plan. If you want to help, God needs you. Just tell Him, "I want to help build the ark, and the thing that I am most concerned about is not what happens to me—what I get out of it—but what happens to the ark and the people who are going to find refuge in it in a little while."

And if you say that, and if you will *do* that, you may find, as Noah did, that the ark you built to save others will be the ark that God will use to carry you and your family safely through the storm!

*If you would like more more copies of this book, or would like
to learn more about Elder Frazee's inspiring 1,660 sermons
in our archives—please use the contact information below:*

WDFsermons.org

support@wdfsermons.org

1-800-WDF-1840 / 706-820-9755

P.O. Box 129

Wildwood, GA 30757

Made in the USA
San Bernardino, CA
28 March 2016